New Perspectives on Site Function and Scale of Cerro de Trincheras, Sonora, Mexico: The 1991 Surface Survey

Maria O'Donovan

Appendixes by
Randall H. McGuire, Maria Elisa Villalpando C.,
Maria O'Donovan, and Jim Holmlund

Arizona State Museum
The University of Arizona®

Arizona State Museum Archaeological Series 195

Arizona State Museum
The University of Arizona
Tucson, Arizona 85721-0026
© 2002 by the Arizona Board of Regents
All rights reserved. Published 2002
Printed in the United States of America

ISBN (paper): 1-889747-73-4

Library of Congress Control Number: 2002105527

ARIZONA STATE MUSEUM ARCHAEOLOGICAL SERIES

General Editor: E. Charles Adams
Technical Editor: Todd Pitezel

The *Archaeological Series* of the Arizona State Museum, The University of Arizona, publishes the results of research in archaeology and related disciplines conducted in the Greater Southwest. Original, monograph-length manuscripts are considered for publication, provided they deal with appropriate subject matter. Information regarding procedures or manuscript submission and review may be obtained from the General Editor, *Archaeological Series*, Arizona State Museum, P.O. Box 210026, The University of Arizona, Tucson, Arizona, 85721-0026; Email: ecadams@u.arizona.edu.

Publication of this volume was made possible by generous grants from the State University of New York, Binghampton and Arizona State Museum, University of Arizona.

Distributed by The University of Arizona Press, 355 S. Euclid Ave., Suite 103, Tucson, Arizona 85719

Cover: Shell turtle from Cerro de Trincheras. Drafted by Victoria Vargas. Courtesy of the Cerro de Trincheras project.

Contents

Figures

Tables

Acknowledgments

This publication would not have been possible without the continued support of several individuals from its original beginning as a dissertation to its current reincarnation. Randy McGuire has continually offered both astute criticism and tireless moral support. For putting up with my blunders, hesitancy, and irritation, I thank him. Susan Pollock and Charles Cobb also deserve thanks for their criticism, suggestions, and support.

A large number of friends and relatives have provided moral support throughout this process. I would especially like to thank LouAnn Wurst for rescuing me several times when I was on the edge and for going above and beyond the call of duty to help me produce the original figures. John McGregor has also lent an ear to me on several occasions. The person that I am most indebted to for making this dissertation a reality is my mother, who has provided countless years of encouragement.

Several people aided me through the technology maze. Luke Willis provided help with information on computer graphics. Sean Rafferty assisted in countless aspects and never got angry over my complete confusion and impatience. Mary Lou Supa drafted figure 3.3 and answered other drafting questions. Nina Versaggi provided me with access to computer equipment, printers, etc. in the Public Archaeology Facility at SUNY-Binghamton and invaluable support. Special thanks goes to Jim Holmlund and his staff for their excellent work on the site map (Figure 4.1) and for rapidly supplying me with various base maps for use in text figures.

The transformation of my original dissertation into this publication was made possible by my sojourn as Visiting Scholar at the Center for Archaeological Investigations, Southern Illinois University at Carbondale. My thanks to all the staff of CAI for making my stay both enjoyable and productive.

The Archaeological Series editors have provided invaluable assistance preparing the manuscript for publication. My thanks go to Charles Adams for reviewing and overseeing the copy and Todd Pitezel for his careful copy editing and comments. I and the editorial staff would like to thank Emiliano Gallaga for graciously translating the abstract.

The assistance I have received throughout this process is immeasurable and this would have been a very different publication without the criticism and input of many colleagues and friends. As always, I alone am responsible for any errors or omissions.

Abstract

The 1991 surface survey of Cerro de Trincheras provides unique insights on site organization that challenge previous explanations of the site type. Functionalist perceptions have dominated explanations of cerros de trincheras and researchers have invoked defensive, ritual, or agricultural needs as a general causal factor in the formation of the site type. Functionalist approaches have prevented archaeologists from exploring the significance of variability and minimized the roles of local history and agency. Detailed examination of spatial patterning at Cerro de Trincheras indicates that it was a complex town with a population that numbered between 1,000 and 2,000 individuals. Cerro de Trincheras hardly fits the criteria of a limited, special purpose site. It was one of the largest towns in the Northwest/Southwest and all of the major specialized functions attributed to cerros de trincheras, including defense, cultivation, and ritual are evidenced here. The multi-scalar, relational approach, developed in this monograph offers an alternative interpretative framework that allows evaluation of the significance of function and variability within the network of social relations pertinent to every site.

Resumen

El recorrido de superficie del sitio Cerro de Trincheras de 1991 proveé un conocimiento profundo sobre la organización del sitio que desafío las interpretaciones previas sobre este. Interpretaciones funcionalistas han dominado las interpretaciones de los sitios cerros de trincheras e investigadores han invocado como factor causal de la formación de estos sitios a necesidades defensivas, rituales y agrícolas. Acercamientos funcionalistas han prevenido a los arqueólogos de explorar la relevancia de la variabilidad y de minimizar el rol de la historia local y de la mediación humana (*agency*). Examinaciones detalladas de patrones espaciales del sitio Cerro de Trincheras indican que fue un pueblo complejo con una población de entre 1,000-2,000 habitantes. Cerro de Trincheras difícilmente cabe en la definición de un sitio con una función limitada y especial. Esté fue una de las poblaciones más grandes dentro del Noroeste/Suroeste y todas las funciones atribuidas a los cerros de trincheras, incluidas defensa, cultivo y ritual, son evidentes en él. El acercamiento relacional y de una escala múltiple, desarrollado en este monograma, ofrece un marco interpretativo alternativo que permite una evaluación de la relevancia de las funciones y de la variabilidad dentro de la red de relaciones sociales pertinente en cada sitio.

Chapter One
Introduction

Cerro de Trincheras is the largest and most diverse cerros de trincheras, a site type that encompasses terraced hill sites located in northern Sonora, northwest Chihuahua, and southern Arizona and New Mexico. The hill setting and terracing of cerros de trincheras have never fit comfortably within the range of characteristics associated with settled village and town life in the region and explanations of the development of the site type have tended to focus on specialized roles. Defensive interpretations have dominated the literature (McGee 1895; Huntington 1912, 1914; Sauer and Brand 1931; Hoover 1941; Fontana et al. 1959; Johnson 1960; Wilcox 1979; Bowen n.d.) and are still quite popular (Wilcox and Haas 1994; Wallace 1995; Roney and Hard 1998; Hard and Roney 1999; LeBlanc 1999) but researchers have also examined agricultural factors (Huntington 1912, 1914; Fontana et al. 1959) and ritual and ideological connotations (Ives 1936; Fontana et al. 1959; Downum 1993) in the development of cerros de trincheras and their "unique" terracing.

The surface survey of Cerro de Trincheras conducted in 1991 is one of a number of recent projects that have established that the largest of these sites were multi-functional villages or towns (McGuire et al. 1993; Downum 1986, 1993; Roney 1996; Hard and Roney 1998a, 1999). This research has redefined conceptual and explanatory parameters by challenging the adequacy of functionalist interpretations. Neither the complexities of daily life on individual cerros de trincheras, nor the variability between sites currently being documented, are illuminated by functional frameworks.

The inherent flaw in functionalist logic as applied to cerros de trincheras is that it privileges broad scale trends or factors in explanation, thus divorcing the sites from the flow of time, culture, and process. The problem here is not function per se, knowing that cerros de trincheras "functioned" as villages or towns is vitally important, but the links drawn between function and causality. Functionalist interpretations range from those that view cerros de trincheras as serving very narrow roles, such as defensive refuges (cf. Johnson 1960; Bowen n.d.; Fontana et al. 1959 [i.e., Black Mountain]; Wilcox 1979; LeBlanc 1999:265), to more moderate positions that focus on a combination of specialized needs with more permanent habitation (Roney and Hard 1998; Hard and Roney 1999) but all embody diminished perspectives on causality, scale, and process. The emphasis on a primary function ultimately roots causality in broad scale factors, minimizing the importance of local processes and human agency, and selectively examines only one aspect at this higher level. In essence, many interpretations reify site function in explanation to the point where it loses significance; it becomes a deterministic factor that impinges on site populations rather than an integral component of the active engagement of these populations with their world.

It is through this engagement that the residents of cerros de trincheras were enmeshed in a complex web of social relations that existed at, and encompassed, multiple temporal and spatial scales (Crumley and Marquardt 1987; Marquardt 1992). The development of specific sites and the site type hinged on the ebb and flow of these relations. Recognizing this leads us to a more complex approach to explanation that incorporates multiple analytical scales and locates causality in the intricate details of the web of relations in which particular site populations were involved.

Multi-scalar, relational approaches require a great deal of data if they are to be done well. This level of data is not available for any cerros de trincheras, including the premier manifestation, Cerro de Trincheras. Systematic research on cerro de trincheras sites only really began in the 1980s, several decades after the basic dimensions of most other site types in the U.S. Southwest were well established. The lack of research on cerros de trincheras in part stems from their "oddity." Viewed as specialized sites outside the typical residential repertoire, they seemed to offer little intellectual challenge or promise.

A less evident reason behind the lack of research on cerros de trincheras lies in their association with "blank" space, a general term for spaces, or cultural areas, that only take on significance in relation to other spaces. The intricacies of local history and development within "blank" spaces are neglected since explanation is routed through a hierarchical framework that privileges other spaces, and when it does address "blank" spaces, only focuses on broad scale issues, patterns, and ties. Much of Northwest Mexico, where most cerros de trincheras are located, has been treated as a "blank" space, sandwiched between the "three little cultures" of the American Southwest and the inherently interesting, highly complex societies to the south. The Gladwinian model of the Hohokam defined an ethnic core-periphery contrast that defined areas where cerros de trincheras occur, such as the Papagueria, as "blank" space, setting the terms of cultural evaluation within the Sonoran Desert area. The Phoe-nix Basin core became the peak of cultural achievement and other areas were measured in terms of this standard. The history of research on the Trincheras Tradition, the cultural area within which Cerro de Trincheras occurs, is largely a chronicle of its definition as a "blank" space in relation to the neighboring Hohokam. Most of the limited prior research conducted on the Trincheras Tradition has been driven by broad scale issues of cultural affiliation and relationships between the two traditions.

The research presented here aims at surpassing the designation of the Trincheras Tradition and cerros de trincheras as "blank" spaces by providing some information on social relations at Cerro de Trincheras. As such it represents an initial step toward building our understanding of this site and how it interacted with, and was shaped by, relations and factors at larger analytical scales. Some of the most significant findings that emerged from the 1991 surface survey concern the scale of the site. Cerro de Trincheras covers 1 km^2 and the main hill, which contains most of the architectural features on the site, rises over 150 meters above the surrounding landscape. Most of the construction effort at the site went into terracing this hill and the approximately 900 terraces that stretch across its surfaces required over 79,000 days of labor (Appendix B). Several hundred other architectural features also represent a significant labor investment by the 1,000-2,000 individuals who lived at Cerro de Trincheras. Cerro de Trincheras is a truly massive site, and it is as large as other major towns in the Northwest/Southwest, such as Snaketown (McGuire et al. 1993:73-74), but it is also much more visually impressive than many. Visual impact is an essential characteristic of monumental constructions and Cerro de Trincheras should be considered such. Its monumental proportions and towering presence appear to have been an integral component of power relations at several scales (McGuire 1998).

THE ARCHAEOLOGICAL CONTEXT

The 1991 Cerro de Trincheras Mapping Project had two primary goals: create a detailed topographic and thematic map of the site and collect a systematic artifact sample that would provide some information on broad scale structure and organization. During the surface survey, field crews recorded over 1,200 architectural features and gathered information on nearly 50,000 artifacts. The analysis and interpretation of these data provided us with the first systematic understanding of a Trincheras cerros de trincheras and aided in the design phase of excavations at the site. After two seasons of excavation (McGuire 1997) and a systematic survey of the area surrounding the site (Fish 1999), Cerro de Trincheras is now one of the best studied examples of the site type. This additional information has in some instances proved useful in reinterpreting the 1991 survey data and evaluating Cerro de Trincheras' place in the region.

Cerro de Trincheras is located in the Rio Magdalena Valley of Sonora and it lies adjacent to this river. The modern Pueblo of Trincheras sits just north of the site between it and the Rio Magdalena. The Trincheras Tradition encompasses the northwestern portion of Sonora, Mexico and a small portion of Arizona near the border town of Nogales. It is bordered on the north by the Hohokam and on the east by the Rio Sonora culture (Figure 1.1).

The Trincheras, Hohokam, and Rio Sonoran cultures comprise three of the five culture areas that cerros de trincheras span (Kirk 1994; Roney 1999). Little is known about the characteristics or distribution of cerros de trincheras in the Rio Sonoran culture and recorded examples are most numerous in the Trincheras, Hohokam and Casas Grandes, or Chihuahuan areas (Kirk 1994; Roney 1999). Cerros de trincheras in the traditional Hohokam area do not extend throughout its en-

tire range and tend to be located in the Tucson Basin and Papagueria (Kirk 1994). In addition, Roney (1999) has recently reported on a possible cerros de trincheras in the Mogollon area.

Cerros de trincheras have an equally impressive temporal range. The earliest known examples date to the Late Archaic and seem to concentrate in Chihuahua (Roney 1996; Hard and Roney 1998a, 1998b, 1999). Recent chronological estimates of A.D. 300-600 for the Tumamoc Hill site in the Tucson basin indicate that other quite early sites exist (Paul Fish personal communication, 1999). Previous evidence had suggested that cerros de trincheras originated in the Trincheras Tradition sometime between A.D. 800-1200 (McGuire and Villalpando 1993) but with continued research we are finding a more complex pattern, including the potential existence of earlier sites in the Trincheras area (Fish 1999). Exotic ceramics recovered during the survey of Cerro de Trincheras suggest that

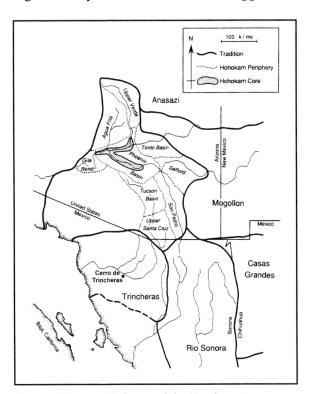

Figure 1.1   Cultures of the Northwest/ Southwest. Courtesy of Randall H. McGuire.

the site was occupied from the thirteenth to fourteenth centuries. Carbon-14 dates from excavations have confirmed that the site principally dates from A.D. 1300-1450 with some minor occupation beginning around A.D. 1250 (McGuire et al. 1999). Other cerros de trincheras in the Tucson Basin date to A.D. 1100-1300, just prior to the main Cerro de Trincheras occupation (Downum et al. 1994).

Given the enormous temporal and spatial ranges of cerros de trincheras, we would expect some morphological and developmental variability related to local culture and relations and changing circumstances. Location on isolated volcanic hills and architectural terraces are the essential defining characteristics of cerros de trincheras but a range of other features are also generally associated with these sites. Circular to square structures are the second most common feature on cerros de trincheras and larger examples of these features are frequently located on site summits. Trails and walls also occur on a number of sites. The occurrence and arrangement of the architectural components of cerros de trincheras varies from site to site (Stacy 1974; Kirk 1994) as does overall site plan. The distribution of more specialized features also appears to exhibit some differences associated with cultural area or time period. For example, large rectangular features that probably served a ritual function are more common on Trincheras Tradition sites and a structural bisecting division that may reflect moiety organization (Downum 1993) occurs on some but not all Hohokam and Trincheras sites (Kirk 1994). Even terrace construction techniques vary to some degree and range from terraces with dry-laid masonry walls, such as at Cerro de Trincheras, to instances where terrace platforms were held in by rock berms (Hard et al. 1999; Hard and Roney 1998a, 1999; Roney 1999)

The large cerros de trincheras from which most of our detailed information on site morphology has come dwarf most known cerros de trincheras, which generally have fewer than fifty terraces (Kirk 1994). This scalar dichotomy is perhaps one of the most important expressions of site type diversity. Some smaller sites seem to have few surface artifacts and in these instances scalar variation may reflect differences in the intensity or duration of site utilization and/or differences in developmental trajectories (Fish 1999).

This brief sketch of Cerro de Trincheras and cerros de trincheras demonstrates two important facts. Archaeological knowledge on cerros de trincheras is still quite limited, an observation that also applies to several of the cultural areas in which the sites occur. The information that does exist suggests that the development of individual cerros de trincheras and the site type was a complex process that varied with local and historical conditions and is fraught with discontinuities. The challenge now facing archaeologists is how to understand the significance of this variability and incorporate it into models and interpretations of the site type.

FUNCTIONALIST AND OTHER DILEMMAS

The strong strain of functionalism that runs through research on cerros de trincheras presents a major obstacle to developing new approaches and interpretations that incorporate diversity and local process and history. Functionalist perceptions transcend theoretical perspectives in this case, uniting early cultural historical work and more recent cultural evolutionary models. In the Trincheras and Hohokam areas, the Gladwinian model became entwined with and reinforced functionalist concepts, adding another interpretative layer that diminished local process.

The prevalence of functionalist concerns throughout the history of research on cerros de trincheras has led to a confusing situation of competing and mutually exclusive interpretations of site function. Agriculture and defense are among the earliest proposed functions for cerros de trincheras (e.g. Huntington 1912, 1914; McGee 1895) that still stimulate research and debate. Huntington's (1914) model focuses on the use of terraces to increase agricultural production, a need brought on by environmental deterioration. Modern approaches to the agricultural use of terraces emphasize micro-climatic variation and the advantages of terraced hillsides in terms of moisture retention and winter cultivation (Katzer 1993; Fish et al. 1984; Downum et al. 1994). In addition, most recent research recognizes that terraces served multiple purposes, including habitation (Fish et al. 1984; Downum et al. 1994).

The extensive literature on defensive utilization of cerros de trincheras (McGee 1895; Sauer and Brand 1931; Hoover 1941; Fontana et al. 1959; Johnson 1960; Wilcox 1979; Bowen n.d.; Gerald 1989; Wilcox and Haas 1994; Wallace 1995; LeBlanc 1999; Roney and Hard 1998; Hard and Roney 1999) has rarely moved beyond rather limited functional assessments and sketchy scenarios of invading groups and ethnic conflict. An interesting exception to this rule is Wilcox's (1979, 1989) theories of Hohokam warfare where cerros de trincheras are seen as a response to the inherent instability of a tributary or alliance system within the Hohokam area. Wilcox's (1979) view of cerros de trincheras as defensive refuges where populations dwelling on the flats would flee during times of attack is one of the most common functional attributions (Johnson 1960; Bowen n.d., Fontana et al. 1959). Cerro de Trincheras has been seen as an exception to this rule (Johnson 1960; Bowen n.d.).

Recent research that has determined that some cerros de trincheras were permanently inhabited villages or towns (McGuire et al. 1993; Downum 1986, 1993) has made the defensive refuge position difficult to sustain and even researchers who favor some defensive role for cerros de trincheras would argue that these were residential sites (Roney and Hard 1998; Hard and

Roney 1999). However, in the wake of this substantial evidence and reevaluation, LeBlanc (1999:265) has revived the defensive refuge interpretation and maintains that at least small cerros de trincheras may have served as refuges. Cerros de trincheras are featured in LeBlanc's (1999) larger overview of warfare in the *American Southwest* simply as evidence of this phenomenon, which he ultimately traces to the interaction of large scale climatic and environmental trends, carrying capacity, and population.

The least developed interpretations of cerros de trincheras center on their connections to ritual, symbolism, and ideology (Ives 1936; Fontana et al. 1959; Haury 1976; Downum 1993). Ives (1936) attributed a symbolic role to a Sonoran cerros de trincheras based on the presence of red mericante lava associated with the Papago (term used in original) god Iitoi and Cerro de Trincheras has been described as a ceremonial site in a functional typology of cerros de trincheras (Fontana et al. 1959). The symbolic aspects of the resemblance of cerros de trincheras to Mesoamerican pyramids have been alluded to by Haury (1976), who suggested that the terracing of the natural hillside was intended to mimic Mesoamerican examples forming a "poor man's pyramid" (Roney 1999). Elaborating on this, Downum (1993) argues that the lack of terraces on fortified sites north of Cerro Prieto in the Tucson Basin implies that cerros de trincheras might be better explained by a model of ideological diffusion rather than one where conditions led to region-wide warfare or agricultural intensification.

The arch of functionalist concerns across varying theoretical perspectives reflects very real and significant questions about why cerros de trincheras were built, how they were utilized, and what roles they played in the prehistory of the Northwest/Southwest. However, the answers to these questions supplied by a primary focus on function are frequently deterministic and reductionist, inhibiting insight into the very issues that they seek to resolve. Arguments that cerros de trincheras principally served any function, whether as agricultural sites, defensive refuges, or defensive habitations, assume a broad unity within the site type that diminishes the appreciation of regional variability and temporal change. This ultimately excludes local contexts and the active role of local populations in explanation. In defensive and agricultural interpretations, site function assumes a causal role connected to broad factors of regional or interregional social instability and/or climatic deterioration (e.g., Huntington 1914; Wilcox 1979, 1989; LeBlanc 1999). At some level, the construction of cerros de trincheras can be seen as an active response to these conditions, but it is a limited response set in motion by broad scale patterns. Local populations would seem to have had very little control over, or impact on, these larger patterns, since they are viewed as affecting a wide area in roughly the same manner, and their subsequent history is largely governed by them. Symbolic and ideological arguments for the role of the site type potentially suffer from the same problems if the reinterpretation of ideology and meaning and its role in local contexts is not considered.

The problems associated with broad scale approaches to the development of cerros de trincheras are equally evident in the Gladwinian model that dominated thought on cultural relationships in the Sonoran Desert region until relatively recently. This ethnic core-periphery model privileges the Phoenix Basin Hohokam as the active source of cultural innovations in the region (Gladwin 1928; Gladwin and Gladwin 1929a, 1933). Populations in regions defined as peripheries are rendered passive receptors and their local sequences of development are essentially shaped by emanations from the core. Originally limited to cerros de trincheras areas in Southern Arizona (Gladwin and Gladwin 1933), the tenets of the model were gradually extended to the bordering Trincheras Tradition through material cul-

ture connections, the most visible being cerros de trincheras. Much of the research on the Trincheras Tradition has focused on its relationship with the Hohokam, glossing over local history, and theories of cerros de trincheras have drawn on elements of this model. Johnson (1960, 1963) invoked Gladwin's (1928) Salado invasion of the Phoenix Basin in his explanation of cerros de trincheras as a defensive response and others have proposed that cerros de trincheras may have sheltered a post-invasion, "degenerate remnant" of the Hohokam (Sauer and Brand 1931). In the absence of the Gladwinian model, there would be no reason to assume that cerros de trincheras arose through tensions between the core and local populations, or that cerros de trincheras were not a product of purely local concerns of a different nature.

Recent research has begun to fill in the "blank" space left in the wake of the Gladwinian model by seeking to fully develop the local context and history of the Trincheras Tradition. It is only with a thorough grasp of local historical sequences that we can evaluate the significance and impact of any broad scale relations and factors, an observation that also applies to the development of cerros de trincheras as a whole. The question of site function has haunted research on cerros de trincheras and, to some extent, prevented archaeological interpretation from moving beyond it. Functionalist concerns have incorporated limited views of causality that obscure local process and may overestimate unity within the site type. Research at several large cerros de trincheras, including Cerro de Trincheras, has revealed that they are residential sites that served multiple functions and on which terraces were used for varying purposes (McGuire et al. 1993; Downum 1986, 1993). Recognition of this fact has severely undermined interpretations of specialized site function and led to the exploration of the complexities of everyday life on these sites. It is essential that we do not subsume our understanding of these complexities under a broad functional label, such as defensive settlement, in larger interpretations of the site type (Roney and Hard 1998; Hard and Roney 1999; Wilcox and Haas 1994; LeBlanc 1999).

A RELATIONAL PERSPECTIVE ON CERRO DE TRINCHERAS AND CERROS DE TRINCHERAS

The general question of why people chose to construct terraced hill side sites that has governed previous research on cerros de trincheras masks a larger series of questions that encompasses temporal and spatial variability, internal organization, and the links between these factors. There may be multiple reasons why people occupied these isolated, volcanic hills and the goal should be to identify and evaluate these reasons within the intricate relational context of particular sites. Decisions that site residents made would have involved their understanding of conditions and social relations at multiple temporal and spatial scales and broad scale factors, such as interregional tensions and warfare, would have developed and played out through internal negotiation and organization (Crumley and Marquardt 1987; Marquardt 1992). In short, function only attains significance when it is rooted in the rhythms of social relations and history.

The multi-scalar approach to landscape advocated by Crumley and Marquardt (1987) offers a non-reductionist analytical framework that can cope with both the particularities of the web of social, material, and ideological relations that people engaged in as well as any similarities of *process* that may pertain to the site type as a whole. The approach does not privilege any temporal or spatial scale in explanation but rather seeks to define scales and analyze their interaction through the dialectics of social relations. As analysis proceeds through various scales, the insights gained regarding relational patterning at each are preserved as much as possible. This framework will provide insight into how any, or several, of the

proposed functions of cerros de trincheras were caught up in the play of social relations that are the source of variability and change and how the significance of these relations may have varied at different scales. While it may not be possible to identify a single, primary function for any site, key social relations and their transformations through time may be identified and examined in the developmental trajectories of particular sites. The insights gained in this process can then be compared to those concerning key relations at other site contexts. The explanations derived from these comparisons will provide a better understanding of the various mechanisms involved in the construction of a long standing, spatially diverse tradition of terraced hill sites and how these are reinterpreted within specific contexts.

This approach requires developing site contexts within a relational framework, rather than fitting a functional mantel to specific contexts. The surface survey of Cerro de Trincheras provides important information on the nature and character of social relations at the site, particularly the role of ritual organization in the creation and maintenance of social inequities. Ritual organization and relations may play a key role in the development of Cerro de Trincheras that has wider implications for power relations within the local settlement system and, perhaps, beyond. In this vein, ritual and symbolic associations of hills, the control of ritual organization and knowledge, and the monumental presence and visual impact of Cerro de Trincheras may have been intricately intermeshed with power relations at multiple scales.

To view Cerro de Trincheras as a monumental site within a cultural landscape, evolutionary views of monumental constructions must be transcended. In this approach, monumental architecture has become one of a series of criteria used to objectively measure social complexity (e.g., Earle 1987; Johnson 1989). Cerro de Trincheras is an ambiguous case in light of the standards of labor investment and centralized planning associated with evolutionary approaches. Total labor investment in the site equals, or exceeds, that of some monumental structures (Muller 1999) but the site does not exhibit strong evidence of centralized planning and there is little reason to think that labor was controlled to any extent. However, it has become increasingly evident that monumental architecture is a poor standard of complexity (e.g., Erasmus 1965; Adams 1967; Earle 1987; Muller 1999) and that rooting the significance of monumental constructions in labor investment and control ignores the dynamics of power relations (Kehoe 2000) and the subjectivity of meaning and symbolism. People have created and given significance to myriad forms of architecture and locations within the landscape through labor, ritual performances, ideology, and meaning. Power is caught up in these contexts through the dynamics of the relations that shaped them. In this sense, the visual impact of monumental constructions, one of their most salient characteristics, is not merely an abstract symbol of power and conspicuous consumption by an elite class (cf. Trigger 1990). Visual impact also conveys some of the specific content and symbolic association involved in the actual dynamics of power. Cerro de Trincheras may be an example of a "cheap" monumental construction but its true significance lies in the ties between the symbolic associations of hills and the social relations that created, and drew on, its powerful presence within the landscape.

SUMMARY

Cerro de Trincheras presents a unique opportunity and a unique challenge for critical re-evaluation and refinement of perspectives on cerros de trincheras and Trincheras prehistory. The results of the analysis of the surface survey data clearly show that Cerro de Trincheras was a complex residential site that should be considered a major town in the Northwest/Southwest. As such, it served many needs for its residential population and the inhabitants of surrounding sites and many roles within the larger context of regional and interregional relations. The succeeding chapters present a reconstruction of the many roles that Cerro de Trincheras played within the multi-scalar network of social relations based on the 1991 survey data. This reconstruction is aimed at stripping away its designation as a "blank" space.

Chapter Two
History of Research on Cerros de Trincheras and the Trincheras Tradition

The history of research on cerros de trincheras sites, and the Trincheras Tradition, is a chronicle of the creation and maintenance of a "blank" space. A "blank" space does not exist independently of other spaces and only gains intellectual priority in relation to these spaces. "Blank" spaces are frequently the result of hierarchical developmental models that privilege one area, or space, as the source of change, creativity, power, etc. (e.g., world systems theory). Such models carry an implicit or explicit core-periphery structure that can be rooted in ethnicity, economic relations, or other factors. Thus, "blank" space is passive space since its history and development are only relevant in relation to core developments. Less is generally known about "blank" spaces than core areas and this lack of information on "blank" spaces only reinforces perceptions of the "active" nature of the core and its superior position.

In this case, the hierarchical structure that would define the Trincheras Tradition as "blank" space originated in the Gladwinian model (see Wilcox 1980:239-40) of the Hohokam. The model established an ethnic core-periphery contrast between the culturally innovative Phoenix Basin core and peripheral and adjoining areas (McGuire 1991). The Gladwins (Gladwin and Gladwin 1933) perceived the Phoenix Basin as a dynamic region of cultural fluorescence and surrounding areas were relegated to an inferior position as passive receptors of core innovations (McGuire 1991). Thus, inferior spaces become effectively "blank" as their real space, or local history, is viewed primarily through the distorted lens of their broad scale relationships with the "superior" culture or area.

"Blank" space is first and foremost a product of prevailing intellectual trends and is subject to changes within the research process. Substantive research within both the peripheries and the core area, as well as theoretical developments within the larger discipline, may intrude upon, and alter, the set pattern of hierarchical explanatory models. These shifts can be traced in the history of Trincheras research from early speculations regarding its relationship to the Hohokam that fed its definition as a "blank" space to a mainstream position that viewed Trincheras as a branch of the Hohokam. This perspective did not remain unchallenged and, with the waning of the cultural historical framework that underlies the Gladwinian model, recent research has sought to understand and explain the Trincheras Tradition within its own terms.

DEFINING "BLANK" SPACE

The shifts in the "blankness" of the Trincheras Tradition reflect a complex research dynamic that is only fully understood by examining its origins and material basis. The research Gladwin (Gladwin 1928; Gladwin and Gladwin 1929a, 1929b, 1930a, 1930b) conducted to establish his Hohokam concept linked a specific set of theoretical assumptions to particular patterns of material culture. This framework formed the basis of the Trincheras Tradition's definition as "blank" space.

Gladwin's (1928) research began with excavations at the impressive site of Casa Grande in the Phoenix Basin and extended to include a series of surveys that radiated out in all directions from the Phoenix Basin area (Gladwin and Gladwin 1929a, 1929b, 1930a, 1930b). The surveys were intended to define the distribution and origins of the culture identified in the Phoenix Basin and its associated Red-on-buff pottery became the major criteria of cultural similarity (Gladwin and Gladwin 1929a, 1929b, 1930a, 1930b). The results of this research led Gladwin and Gladwin (1933:5) to one central conclusion that neatly summarizes the basic tenets of the Gladwinian model:

> In all directions, contact was established with peoples who, at the time of the Colonial period, were in a less advanced stage of development, and the belief has grown that the tide of civilization flowed outward from the Hohokam to affect peripheral areas, rather than that the Hohokam acquired their civilization from an exterior source (Gladwin and Gladwin 1933:5).

The underlying assumptions that form the basis of the Gladwinian model are clearly illustrated by this quote and rest in part in Gladwin's research process. Gladwin started from an assumption that Phoenix Basin core development was the norm and evaluated adjacent areas by their degree of similarity to this standard. This framework made departures from core patterns of material culture in peripheral areas an aberration that had to be explained. By equating differences in material culture and developmental trajectories with cultural lag and inferiority in the peripheries, Gladwin established the temporal and spatial pattern of "civilization" within the region and ensuing core-centric conceptual frameworks and research agendas (McGuire 1991).

Gladwin and Gladwin's (1929a) brief statements regarding the Trincheras area give few indications as to how they would have classified it but it seems they would have considered it a separate tradition rather than a periphery of the Phoenix Basin Hohokam (McGuire 1991:358). However, they did define an area of southeastern Arizona and northwestern Sonora known as the Papagueria as a periphery (Gladwin and Gladwin 1933). The Papagueria and the Tucson Basin are the two areas within the perceived Hohokam periphery where cerros de trincheras sites occur. The presence of cerros de trincheras sites established a material link between the Trincheras Tradition and a defined Hohokam periphery that aided the extension of the theoretical premises of the Gladwinian model to the Trincheras Tradition.

In this same vein, later researchers (Sauer and Brand 1931; Haury 1950; Johnson 1963) would also apply Gladwin and Gladwin's (1929a) two theories of Papaguerian development, or rather its failure in relation to the core, to explain the Trincheras Tradition. The first theory views Papaguerian prehistory as a period of stagnation by remnant populations that had been pushed out of the more desirable Phoenix Basin by the approach of the "Polychrome People" (Gladwin and Gladwin 1929a:128). At the time, Gladwin and Gladwin (1929a:129) seem to have favored the second explanation—that Papaguerian populations were a portion of the original colonizing population whose "development was retarded" by the inhospitable environment they occupied (Gladwin and Gladwin 1929a:129). This "developmentally retarded" theory better explained the Colonial period Red-on-buff sherds at some Classic period sites, which they saw as indicative of early stagnation and separation from main stream developments in the Papagueria (Gladwin and Gladwin 1929a:129).

Other recognized material similarities between the Trincheras Tradition and the Hohokam culture also acted to reinforce and maintain the Trincheras Tradition's incorporation into the Gladwinian model. Populations in the Trincheras area produced shell artifacts that are very similar in appearance to Hohokam items but were made using a different technique (Woodward 1936:121; Haury 1976:306). Early notions of the shell exchange network placed Trincheras in the role of suppliers of raw shell and unfinished artifacts (Brand 1938; Johnson 1960), or finished artifacts (Sauer and Brand 1931:113-114; Woodward 1936:117) to the Hohokam. Recent frameworks limit Trincheras involvement to specific time periods (Bowen n.d.), or areas (McGuire and Howard 1987:121). There are also certain stylistic parallels between both cultural traditions. Trincheras Purple-on-red ceramics show some stylistic similarities to Hohokam ceramics (McGuire 1991:356) as does rock art (Lindauer and Zaslow 1994; Hayden 1972).

A more ambiguous source of connections between Trincheras and Hohokam involves Mesoamerican affiliations. The possibility of a Mesoamerican origin for the Hohokam took on a more serious character when Haury (1976:351-353) came out in favor of the proposition. Any migration of people would have had to pass through northwest Mexico and the search for the route has lead some researchers to the Trincheras area (Haury 1976:352).

The substantive connections—cerros de trincheras sites, shell production and exchange, stylistic parallels and Mesoamerican associations—suggest that broad scale interaction between the Hohokam and Trincheras areas is a significant issue. However, none of the substantive data indicate a direction to the flow of information and items or a hierarchical relationship between the two areas. In the absence of the connections between specific patterns of material culture and position within a developmental hierarchy established by the Gladwinian model, researchers might have interpreted these material connections in a more neutral manner.

The structure of inquiry that defined the Trincheras Tradition as a "blank" space has had both positive and negative effects on substantive research. Most research conducted in the Trincheras area until the 1980s drew inspiration from the hierarchical tenets of the Gladwinian model. Archaeologists who came to the Trincheras Tradition interested more in broad scale issues of cultural connection and interaction with the Hohokam produced layer upon layer of information that gradually filled in some of this "blank" space. However, these researchers primarily sponsored expansive surveys and limited excavations. This type of work provided some information on material culture useful for examining parallels between the two areas but very little depth on issues of local development.

More than three hundred years after the "discovery" of the Trincheras area, and more than one hundred years after the first scientific expeditions, a comprehensive time-space framework for the Trincheras Tradition does not exist. It is still largely a "blank" space in substance, even if it is no longer considered so in theory. The depth of knowledge on most cerros de trincheras sites is comparable to that of the Trincheras Tradition and much previous work has tended to derive interpretations of the site type from relatively brief surface observations.

DISCOVERING "BLANK" SPACE

Cerros de trincheras sites were "discovered" twice. The written record begins with the Spanish conquest. These accounts are followed over 100 years later by Anglos exploring the "unknown" west. Cerro de Trincheras attracted particular attention in these accounts due to its sheer magnitude. Nevertheless, early explorers spent little time at Cerro de Trincheras and some did not even bother to ascend the hill. The appearance of the site, with its distinctive rock walled terraces and hill setting, most intrigued early visitors and formed the basis of any explanations. These explanations contain the first suppositions regarding the significance of site function.

The Spanish record begins with Juan Mateo Manje's (Burrus 1971:178) visit to Cerro de Trincheras in 1694 during one of Kino's exploratory expeditions. His brief account of the site is the source of the term Trincheras, which he used to describe the "fortifications" on the site. Manje (Burrus 1971:178) counted 100 of these terraces from his position on the valley floor. He derived his defensive interpretation of the site from local accounts of the defensive use of the site, specifically involving a "parade ground" at the crest where residents would use the terraces to hold back invaders. Defensive use of cerros de trincheras was also recorded during the ethnohistoric period by a Spanish Jesuit missionary, Ignaz Pfefferkorn. Pfefferkorn extended the ethnohistoric use of cerros de trincheras by the Pima and Seri during the 1750s in their revolts against Spanish colonial rule to his interpretation of their prehistoric role as defensive habitations for the Pima, Opata, and Seri (Pfefferkorn 1990:152-154, 207).

Anglo explorers and researchers started venturing into Sonora during the late nineteenth century. Their reasons for coming were varied, from economic exploration to climatic interpretation, but all sought to chart the little known space that lay "at the door of the great empire of Yankee enterprise" (Lumholtz 1912:vii). Two brief accounts of Cerro de Trincheras by "armchair archaeologists" describe it as a fortification (Schumacher 1881) or an Aztec ruin (Hamilton 1883). Later accounts were based on actual examination of the site.

W.J. McGee spent four days at Cerro de Trincheras and the adjacent site of Trincheritas in November of 1895 during the Bureau of American Ethnology expedition to the Seri (McGee 1895:350, 1896:983). McGee's (2000 [1895]:62-64) description of Cerro de Trincheras mentions several features for the first time including circular stone structures, which he interpreted as house circles, El Caracol on the crest, and bedrock metates. The expedition also drew and photographed some of the petroglyphs and mapped both sites (McGee 2000 [1895]:62-64). In a summary article McGee (1895:372-373) interpreted cerros de trincheras as defensive sites related to invaders from the high Sierra Madre.

Carl Lumholtz received a commission to ascertain the economic potential of the Papagueria, and traveled extensively in this area from 1909 to 1910. His popular account of his travels describes Cerro de Trincheras as having twenty terraces and circular stone structures on the summit, an observation that, along with his artifact descriptions, was based on his Mexican informants (Lumholtz 1912:141). Lumholtz (1912:142) ascribed distinct functional associations to Cerro de Trincheras and other cerros de trincheras in Sonora and Arizona, where he thought terraces probably served as fortifications for a population living on the summit. He rejected an exclusively defensive interpretation for Cerro de Trincheras by reference to the exposed southern side of the hill and also found agricultural explanations of terraces inadequate due to the extensive habitation debris on them. Instead, he interpreted this seemingly inexplicable site as a ceremonial center that also served defensive needs (Lumholtz 1912:142).

Huntington (1910, 1914:67-70) offers the best description of Cerro de Trincheras during this period and his intense interest may have stemmed from his research topic. Huntington (1914:3-4), a geographer, came to the arid southwest to investigate his theories on the effect of climate on human history. He spent roughly one and a half days exploring and mapping Cerro de Trincheras as part of his observations on the distribution of prehistoric sites, including other cerros de trincheras, within his study area (Huntington 1910).

Cerro de Trincheras was a multi-functional settlement in Huntington's (1914:67-70) opinion, serving religious (La Cancha), military (El Caracol and circular stone structures), and agricultural (terraces) needs. His interpretation of the agricultural function of terraces contradicts Lumholtz's (1912:142) and our observations on the extent of habitation debris. He argued that terraces not only lacked domestic trash deposits but were also not large enough to have supported habitation structures. The resemblance of these sites to terraced agricultural areas in Asia and the favorable slope position of the terraces for agriculture strengthened this negative evidence. Huntington ascribed the need for increased agricultural production to population pressure and climatic deterioration or the cultivation of special crops, specifically grapes (Huntington 1914:67-70).

The agricultural and defensive aspects of cerros de trincheras supported Huntington's (1914) broader thesis on environmental determinism. He concluded that climatic shifts producing reduced rainfall, possibly accompanied by overpopulation, had lead to a period of famine and warfare (Huntington 1914:73-74). Huntington's (1914:67) other notable observation concerns his views on the cultural affiliation of Cerro de Trincheras. He believed the site belonged to a branch of the culture in southern Arizona that he termed the Hohokam.

Early accounts of cerros de trincheras seem highly speculative to modern archaeologists but they introduced some of the main threads of contemporary debate. Terracing made cerros de trincheras truly "unique" and early explorers sought their explanations in terrace function. With little information on which to draw, they relied primarily on "common sense" in their interpretations. Defensive interpretations are still made for cerros de trincheras (Wilcox 1979; Wilcox and Haas 1994; LeBlanc 1999; Roney and Hard 1998; Hard and Roney 1999) and interest has renewed in Huntington's (1914) agricultural associations (Fish et al. 1984; Downum 1986; Katzer 1993; Downum et al. 1994). It was Huntington (1914:67) who first applied the term Hohokam to the cultural remains in southern Arizona and the

Trincheras area and as research progressed the cultural relationships between the core Hohokam area and their southern neighbors would form one of the main issues of debate.

CLASSIFYING "BLANK" SPACE

The next major period of work on cerros de trincheras sites came during the late 1920s and early 1930s as researchers attempted to refine cultural definitions and gather more systematic data on cerros de trincheras. Research was inaugurated by Frank Midvale, who undertook a survey of the Papagueria for the Gladwins that extended to just below the modern Pueblo of Trincheras. Midvale's survey, which focused on collecting ceramic information, is primarily remarkable for providing the basis for the "degenerate remnant" and "developmentally retarded" explanations of Papaguerian prehistory (Gladwin and Gladwin 1929a:128-129). The real "stars" of this cultural construction period are a pair of geographers who took serious umbrage with Huntington's (1912, 1914) theories of environmental determinism.

Sauer and Brand (1931) undertook an extensive survey of Sonora to gather data to refute Huntington (1912, 1914). Their argument against environmental determinism and degradation in late prehistory is a prime example of academic testiness. Sauer and Brand (1931:93) traced contemporary aridity to over-grazing and erosion cycles that started in the nineteenth century. One of the pieces of evidence cited in their argument was the presence of a cienaga at Trincheras within living memory (Sauer and Brand 1931:93). Discounting the evidence of prehistoric environmental deterioration by documenting its historical development removed the lynch pin of Huntington's (1912, 1914) argument.

Sauer and Brand (1931:121) specifically challenged Huntington's (1914) interpretations of cerros de trincheras. They claimed that terraces consisted of a rubble core with a thin layer of soil over it, making them useless for agricultural purposes (Sauer and Brand 1931:121). This observation was based only on surface examination. Sauer and Brand's (1931:114-119) alternative interpretation fell back on defense, and although they found no clear evidence of what they considered could be dwellings, they believed that surface artifact densities did indicate habitation at cerros de trincheras.

Sauer and Brand (1931) offered the first definition of Trincheras culture, which focused on relationships with the Hohokam. Their brief description of cultural traits describes Trincheras as a group centered along the Magdalena and Altar drainages occupying both the valley floors and cerros de trincheras. Trincheras populations produced a distinctive pottery type, Trincheras Purple-on-red, and unique architectural features including rock-walled terraces and "corrals" (Sauer and Brand 1931:107-109, 117-118). The term corrals is commonly used to refer to circular structures and summit features found on cerros de trincheras. Sauer and Brand (1931:117-119) designated the Trincheras area as a sub-culture of the Hohokam and in this they followed the Gladwins' (Gladwin and Gladwin 1929a:119-121, 128-129) theories on Papaguerian development. Sauer and Brand suggest that the Trincheras culture may have been a remnant of the Hohokam (Red-on-buff culture) that survived into Pueblo IV times under hostile attack from invaders, the Opata and Pima, who eventually became the Tohono O'odham (Sauer and Brand 1931:118-119). This explanation of Trincheras origins and development is a variant of the Gladwins' (Gladwin and Gladwin 1929a:128-129) "degenerate remnant" theory. In places, Sauer and Brand (1931:107-109, 117-119) seem to concede that their explanation would have differed if not for the Gladwins' (Gladwin and Gladwin 1929a:119-121) ceramic classification

placing Trincheras pottery between Red-on-buff and historic Papago wares. However, the Trincheras culture was now branded as the dying and degenerate remnants of the Hohokam and, within this framework, could never exist or develop on its own.

In a later article, Brand (1935:300) refined some aspects of the initial definition of the Trincheras culture, primarily concentrating on the decorated pottery types of Trincheras P/r and Trincheras (Nogales) Polychrome. He also retracted the cultural affiliations proposed in the previous article (Sauer and Brand 1931) and proposed that Trincheras developed independently during Pueblo III. The material culture differences that suggested this cultural independence potentially stemmed from a state of hostilities between the two populations (Brand 1935:300).

The subject of Hohokam-Trincheras relationships also occupied Woodward (1936) in his examination of La Playa (Boquillas in Sauer and Brand [1931:93]) near Cerro de Trincheras. Woodward (1936) compiled some of the basic information on Trincheras shell that Haury (1976) later drew on to differentiate the Hohokam and Trincheras shell industries. Shell artifacts from both cultures are very similar in appearance but are produced using different manufacturing techniques (Woodward 1936:121; Haury 1976:306; McGuire and Howard 1987:120). Trincheras bracelet manufacturing techniques yield a shell blank primarily produced by abrasion, while Hohokam artisans used what has been described as a chipping method (Haury 1976:306) to achieve a rough bracelet form. The technical differences in Hohokam and Trincheras shell production were not apparent at the time and Woodward (1936:117) proposed that La Playa was a major manufacturing center for shell ornaments or bracelet blanks that were traded north into the Hohokam area. Woodward (1936) also argued that stylistic parallels between Hohokam shell and Mesoamerican crafts indicated that the Hohokam, and perhaps by extension their Trincheras suppliers, ultimately originated in Mesoamerica.

Several limited survey and excavation projects in Arizona and Sonora also added to the growing body of knowledge on cerros de trincheras. Gordon Ekholm's (1937, 1939) expansive survey of Sonora and parts of Sinaloa included a brief stop at Cerro de Trincheras in 1937 (Ekholm 1937:4). He also recorded other cerros de trincheras sites throughout Sonora. Ekholm's subsequent research concentrated in the Guasave region of Sinaloa and he never reported on his findings in Sonora to any great extent. Also in Sonora, Ives (1936) investigated a small cerro de trincheras near Quitovaquita that consisted of a single wall, or possibly a terrace, 300 feet (91m) long. Ives (1936:259) suggested that the site was used for religious purposes based on the occurrence of red mericante lava, which is associated by the Tohono O'odham with the god Iitoi.

Investigations at cerros de trincheras in Arizona concentrated on Papaguerian sites. Fraps' (1936) work at Blackstone Ruin focused on the 114 circular rooms she documented at the site. Test excavations performed on forty of these rooms suggested to her that they were not used on a permanent basis and she interpreted one with an open side as a windbreak. Artifact density in the rooms and across the site was low and, in most cases, depth to caliche was shallow, less than 10 inches (25 cm). However, Fraps (1936) excluded defense, which has become the most prevalent interpretation for intermittently occupied cerros de trincheras with "wind breaks," based on the easy approach to the site (see Fontana et al. 1959).

Hoover (1941) investigated seven cerros de trincheras on the Tohono O'odham Reservation, and confirmed the existence of two more near the international border in Sonora, from which he compiled a description of standard traits. Hoover's (1941:231, 236) interpretations emphasized defense and his use of the term reserve villages implies sporadic occupation dependent on the state of hostilities, although he did identify terraces and circular stone structures as habitation areas. In his contribution to the debate over terrace function, he pointed out that Papaguerian sites were located near favorable bajada land that was more likely to be used for agricultural production than terraces (Hoover 1941:236).

In his explanation of cerros de trincheras Hoover (1941) rejected Gladwin's (Gladwin et al. 1938) view of cultural relationships and replacements in the Sonoran Desert. The expanded theories Gladwin (Gladwin et al. 1938) developed after the excavations at Snaketown now identified the invaders with the polychrome pots as the Salado, who conquered the indigenous Hohokam at the start of the Classic period. Salado populations then retreated to the east and southeast after A.D. 1400, leaving a remnant Hohokam population to become the ethnohistoric Pima (Gladwin et al. 1938:14-18). While accepting Gladwin's version of events in the Phoenix Basin, Hoover (1941:237-238) refused to entertain an extension of this interpretation that would associate cerros de trincheras with Tohono O'odham resistance to the invading Salado. Instead, he proposed cerros de trincheras stemmed from a general period of unrest following the great drought at the end of the thirteenth century (Hoover 1941:238). Hoover (1941:237-238) seems to have leaned towards the position that Papaguerian sites were occupied by poor, or inferior, subgroups of the Trincheras culture, which may have led him to focus less on Hohokam connections. However, he admitted that the question of cultural affiliation was complicated by the use of cerros de trincheras by Tohono O'odham populations. His concession, that the sites were built and used by several different cultures, was insightful, although perhaps not appropriate in this context.

The initial classificatory period of research is characterized by the first substantial attempts to interpret cultural relationships in the Sonoran desert. The Gladwins' (Gladwin and Gladwin 1929a, 1933; Gladwin et al. 1938) perspectives significantly influenced these attempts from the first definition of the Trincheras Tradition (i.e., Sauer and Brand 1931) to larger issues regarding the role of cerros de trincheras in Northwest/Southwest prehistory (e.g., Hoover 1941). The Gladwins' (Gladwin and Gladwin 1929a, 1933; Gladwin et al. 1938) proposals were not accepted wholesale and uncritically (e.g., Hoover 1941:228), as some of the commentary in Sauer and Brand (1931:107-109) and Brand (1935) highlights, but these tentative divergences had very little impact on larger assumptions of underlying cultural ties between Trincheras and Hohokam.

RECLASSIFYING "BLANK" SPACE

What I have termed the reclassification of the Trincheras Tradition encompasses a period during which Haury (1950) and Di Peso (1956) offered competing explanations for divergent cultural patterns south of the Hohokam core. The debate hinged on contrasting interpretations of cultural continuity between the core and peripheries in the Pioneer to Colonial time span. Haury (1950) saw sufficient continuity between the Papagueria and the core Phoenix Basin to assert that they were different branches of the same culture that increasingly diverged through time due to variation in environmental conditions. Di Peso's (1956) work in the Santa Cruz Valley convinced him that patterning here was significantly different from that of the Phoenix Basin core and that the Hohokam were invaders. Ethnic conflict began when the original Pioneer Period culture that he termed the O'otam (O'odham) was invaded and subjugated by the Hohokam during the Colonial period.

The position of the Trincheras culture in these theories was consistent with each author's view of events in southern Arizona. In a footnote to the Ventana Cave report, Haury (1950:546-548) proposed that the Trincheras area belonged to the desert branch of the Hohokam that he had defined in the Papagueria. The desert branch harkened

back to Gladwin's "developmentally retarded" theory (Gladwin and Gladwin 1929a:119) and essentially associated an inferior cultural expression with a marginal area. Di Peso (1956:360) seems to have associated Trincheras with O'otam (O'odham), the original population in the region, based on his identification of stylistic and manufacturing similarities between Trincheras ceramics and his Upper Pima, or O'otam (O'odham) series (McGuire 1991). Both men noted (Di Peso 1956; Haury 1950:353) that Trincheras ceramics primarily occurred in Colonial-Sedentary contexts in the Hohokam area, which Di Peso (1956) took as an indication that exchange between the Hohokam and Trincheras in shell, 3/4 grooved axes, and other items ended after the O'otam (O'odham) expelled the Hohokam invaders. Haury (1950:353) read this as evidence of the extinction of Trincheras populations prior to the fourteenth century.

Lack of data was a limiting factor for both perspectives and Di Peso and Haury encouraged separate projects in Sonora. Di Peso sent Hinton (1955) to survey the Altar Valley based on his assumption that it was the center of Trincheras culture. Haury's student Johnson (1960, 1963) worked at La Playa, which was noted for its large quantities of shell (Woodward 1936).

Hinton (1955) spent six weeks surveying the Altar Valley during the summer of 1954, from which he produced initial site and ceramic typologies and a four period chronological framework (Hinton 1955:2-10). The chronology lacks any defined pre-ceramic manifestations, with Period 1 extending from A.D. 700-1200. Cerros de trincheras belong to the succeeding period (about A.D. 1200-contact [late seventeenth to early eighteenth centuries]), which is poorly defined chronologically and Hinton (1955:10) concedes that a few sites could pre-date Period 1. The two remaining periods cover ethnohistoric and historic occupation of the valley from the seventeenth to twentieth centuries (Hinton 1955:10-11).

Johnson (1960:2, 1963) spent weekends at La Playa, a large floodplain site near Cerro de Trincheras, and at one of two adjacent cerros de trincheras for several months conducting excavations and surface survey. La Playa is vast and would take years of intensive research to adequately document but Johnson (1960, 1963) did produce some initial descriptive data and interpretations.

Excavations at the cerros de trincheras site included eight test pits placed within circular rock structures that produced no artifacts below ground surface. Johnson (1960:42) also noted that surface scatter on the site was very light. He suggested that these smaller cerros de trincheras were defensive refuges but saw Cerro de Trincheras as a unique example of the site type with dense surface artifact scatter indicative of permanent occupation (Johnson 1960:45, 1963:179).

In his conclusions regarding La Playa and Trincheras culture, Johnson (1960:220-225) did not depart significantly from Haury's position, which represented mainstream research in the Sonoran desert. The cultural similarities he saw, particularly parallels in ceramics and cerros de trincheras, could only mean that the Trincheras Tradition was another manifestation of the desert branch of the Hohokam. His belief that Papaguerian cerros de trincheras within the previously defined desert branch (Haury 1950) represented resistance to a Salado invasion of the core was marshaled to support his assignment of Trincheras to the desert branch (Johnson 1963:184). Johnson's other notable observations also involve cultural stagnation and Hohokam ties. He dated La Playa to roughly A.D. 800-1100 using cross-dated Trincheras ceramics, a determination that led him to interpret the Trincheras lithic industry as conservative due to its similarity with its Cochise roots (Johnson 1960:220-225). (Johnson was almost certainly wrong about La Playa representing a single occupation, which underlies his erroneous view of the lithic industry.) Johnson (1960:220-225) also sug-

gested that Trincheras supplied raw shell to the Hohokam. Haury (1976) later cited Johnson's work in his argument against Trincheras as a major supplier of shell bracelet blanks and artifacts.

Very little other research was conducted during the immediate post-war period. Our knowledge of the adjacent Seri culture in Sonora grew with Hayden's (1956) survey of the central coast and Fontana and others (1959) constructed a functional typology of cerros de trincheras based on their survey of Black Mountain in Arizona. The typology consists of four types: defensive, ceremonial, agricultural, and habitation. Defensive sites have little material culture, stone walls, and bastions with Black Mountain representing a typical example. The primary difference between defensive and ceremonial sites is the abundance of petroglyphs but the category is also based on ethnohistoric usage and notions of visual parallels between cerros de trincheras and Mesoamerican temple mounds. Cerros de trincheras that could have served ceremonial functions include Martinez Hill and Cerro de Trincheras. The necessary constituents of habitation are dwellings and abundant material culture, such as at the Gila Bend site. The agricultural type is a tentative one, as no examples of exclusively agricultural sites had, or have, been recorded (Fontana et al. 1959:51).

The lasting significance of the ethnic attribution debate lies in the revisionist possibilities of Di Peso's (1956) work and the new data on the Trincheras area it generated. Di Peso (1956) presented an alternative view of ethnic relationships that imputed an active role to perceived Hohokam peripheries that would extend to the Trincheras area. The potential of Di Peso's (1956) challenge to the core-periphery model of the Hohokam was somewhat muted by his general theoretical similarities with Haury. Both worked within the then dominant cultural historical approach and assumed a direct correlation between material culture and ethnicity but each read the record differently. Resolution of the debate rested on substantial and unambiguous material evidence, which each may have thought he would find in Sonora.

"BLANK" SPACE AS MIGRATORY PASSAGEWAY

The Trincheras area enjoyed a brief interlude as "blank" space between the Hohokam and Mesoamerica. Haury's (1976) second set of excavations at Snaketown produced strong evidence of a Pioneer to Colonial Period continuum that undermined Di Peso's invasion theory of the Hohokam, at least in the Phoenix Basin. It was also here that Haury (1976:352) became convinced that the Hohokam had migrated into the area from Mesoamerica at the start of the Pioneer Period. A new researcher, Wasley, now set out for Sonora in search of the migratory trail that the Hohokam took out of Mesoamerica to the Southwest.

Wasley's (1968) survey of Sonora concentrated primarily on the western coastal areas. As a result of this work, Wasley (1968) defined three major cultural complexes in Sonora: Trincheras, a coastal complex roughly representing the ethnohistoric Seri, and the rest of Sonora. The Trincheras Tradition, as he defined it, extended from Puerto Peñasco (Rocky Point) east to Nogales and from there south to Carbo, approximately 40 miles north of Hermosillo. On the west it embraced the Rio San Miguel River Valley. Wasley (1968) recorded four different types of sites in the Trincheras area: 1) agricultural villages with canals, 2) cerros de trincheras, 3) camp sites, and 4) petroglyph sites. The major quest of the expedition, the migration route of the Hohokam, went unfulfilled (Haury 1976:352) but it did result in the first major chronological framework for the Trincheras Tradition which was compiled by Bowen (n.d.).

Bowen's (n.d.) cultural framework attempted to refine the broad outlines of settlement pattern within the Trincheras Tradition. To accomplish this,

he defined four ecological zones: 1) the major river valleys—the Altar, Concepcion, Magdalena and San Miguel; 2) the mouth of the Concepcion River defined as a separate zone within the river valley zone; 3) coastal settings; and 4) interior regions.

The four-stage chronology he developed (Bowen n.d.) begins with the Initial Stage, which roughly corresponds to the Archaic period Cochise Culture. Isolationist Stage (A.D. 300-800) sites are primarily differentiated from the previous stage by the addition of Trincheras P/r ceramics. Lithic technology is relatively unchanged from the previous stage, implying a fairly conservative lithic tradition, an idea first proposed by Johnson (1960, 1963). Sites of the Isolationist Stage predominately occur in the coastal and interior zones. Trincheras P/br and Trincheras Polychrome are typically associated with Receptionist Stage (A.D. 800-1300) sites. La Playa, with its shell jewelry industry, and other large village sites in major drainages, date primarily to this time period. The introduction of shell jewelry manufacture raises the specter of Trincheras-Hohokam interaction and Bowen (n.d.:160-161) believed that connections between the two were probably initiated during the Receptionist Stage. The Hohokam provided the inspiration for the "lesser" artisans of the Trincheras, hence the name of this stage. Late Stage sites are also located primarily within the fluvial zone of major drainages and date from A.D. 1300-1450 (Bowen n.d.:134-144). Bowen (n.d.:139) proposed that cerros de trincheras sites were introduced during this period and that local production of painted ceramics might have been seriously curtailed.

Bowen's (n.d.) comments on cerros de trincheras sites in his chronological summary initially seem to support an interpretation similar to that presented in the functional typology, which acknowledges differentiation in functional roles (Fontana et al. 1959:51). However, his discussions focus on cerros de trincheras as defensive refuges, with Cerro de Trincheras as a special exception that may have been inhabited on a permanent basis late in its history. Bowen (n.d.:183) also suggests that some cerros de trincheras were used to resist a possible protohistoric Piman invasion, an idea that echoed Sauer and Brand's (1931) early work. These invaders may have forced Trincheras populations into the Papagueria where they merged with existing occupants forming a new cultural tradition, presumably the Tohono O'odham (Bowen n.d:187).

The research in the Trincheras region inspired by Haury's (1976) search for the migratory route of the Hohokam produced a more systematic chronology with a settlement and environmental focus (Bowen n.d.) but did little to alter perceptions of the Trincheras Tradition. Bowen's (n.d.) chronological summary is dependent on broad relationships for its framework and tinged with passive terminology, as exemplified in the Receptionist Stage, that reflects the inferior status of the Trincheras culture. These perceptions have only been dispelled within the last fifteen years.

ENDING "BLANK" SPACE

The end of "blank" space can only come by abandoning broad scale theories and models that treat the Trincheras region as a periphery in the true sense of the word—an area devoid of cultural and historical innovation—and that extend this status to the cultural manifestations, such as cerros de trincheras, within it. To fully end the "blankness" of the Trincheras Tradition, we also need to build local contexts through the in-depth substantive research that has long been neglected. The multi-phase project on Cerro de Trincheras of which this report is one small part has undertaken these goals, supplying us with new data on local history that can frame our understanding of broad scale issues and relations. Several substantial research projects on cerros de trincheras in southern Arizona and Chihuahua (Downum 1986, 1993; Downum et al. 1994; Roney 1996; Hard and Roney 1998a, 1999) are also making major con-

tributions to our knowledge of the one of the most visible manifestations of local process and broad scale connections.

The Centro Regional de Noroeste, Instituto Nacional de Antropología e Historia (INAH), in Hermosillo has been responsible for much of the work undertaken in Sonora within the last twenty years. The Centro has recorded sites in the region and published a list of known sites and who recorded them (Braniff and Quijada 1978). In addition, Braniff (1978) has published on the archaeology of the Rio San Miguel valley, including the cerros de trincheras sites found there. These concentrate in the lower and middle portions of the valley and seemingly lack Trincheras P/r pottery, supporting Hinton's (1955) and Bowen's (n.d.) conclusions that the sites post-date the pottery type (Braniff 1978:77, 81).

Stacy (1974, 1977) compiled some information on Sonoran cerros de trincheras for a morphological comparison with five sites she mapped and surface collected in the Baboquivari Valley in the Arizona Papagueria. Her morphological typology consists of three classes. Type I sites only have encircling rock walls near the summit, while Type II sites also have terraces below the summit. Cerro de Trincheras would fall into the Type II category. The third category contains sites that have walls, or terraces, on one or two faces of the hill, or terracing only around a hill peak (Stacy 1974:177-179). The advantage of this typology is that it carries none of the functional assumptions associated with other classifications (e.g., Fontana et al. 1959:51). However, Stacy's (1974) failure to link morphological variability to larger substantive issues means that the typology provides little insight into the organization of the site type or the basis for variability. The range of activities she lists for the sites, based in part on historic analogy, runs the gamut from defense through subsistence and habitation (Stacy 1974:190-205).

Research focused on the Trincheras Tradition includes McGuire and Villalpando's (1993) multi-phase project. The ground work for this project was laid in 1984 by an expansive automotive survey of the Magdalena, Concepcion, and Altar drainages, during which several cerros de trincheras were recorded and sketch mapped (McGuire 1985; survey notes on file at SUNY-Binghamton and Consejo de Arqueología, INAH, Mexico City). The first phase of the project entailed a systematic survey of the Altar Valley (McGuire and Villalpando 1993), which was followed by the present research at Cerro de Trincheras in the Rio Magdalena Valley (McGuire et al. 1993; McGuire et al. 1999).

The Altar Valley survey documented 98 sites from Early Archaic to historic Tohono O'odham time periods, including eleven cerros de trincheras. The broad outlines of settlement pattern within the valley show an increase in the types and number of sites during McGuire and Villalpando's (1993) Altar Phase (approximately A.D. 800-1300), during which most habitation sites are located in the floodplain. This pattern shifts in the subsequent El Realito Phase, which encompasses the fourteenth and fifteenth centuries, when there is a decline in the number and variety of sites, although many sites increase in size. Habitation contexts also change and these sites now occur primarily in terrace areas (McGuire and Villalpando 1993:71). Cerros de trincheras first appear during the Altar Phase and continue into the El Realito Phase, although they decline in size and artifact density (McGuire and Villalpando 1993:71). The largest cerro de trincheras contained 43 terraces and most cerros de trincheras seem to have been habitation sites. Nine sites had an average artifact density very close to that of valley floor habitation sites, while the two remaining sites had low surface artifact densities that suggest other uses. Few cerros de trincheras are associated with pit house villages, which casts serious doubt on the defensive refuge interpretation (McGuire and Villalpando 1993:66).

One of the major goals of the Altar Valley project was chronology. McGuire and Villalpando's (1993:57-65) chronology essentially follows the broad outlines of Bowen's (n.d.) summary, although they place the timing of some events, such as the appearance of cerros de trincheras sites and shell jewelry production, earlier and include three protohistoric or ethnohistoric phases. Braniff's (1985) data would suggest that both chronological summaries are inaccurate in their assignment of an end date prior to the fourteenth century for Trincheras P/r ceramics. She has suggested that the ceramic type and the cultural patterns associated with it continued until Spanish contact, based on fifteenth century C-14 dates for contexts containing Trincheras P/r.

McGuire's and Villalpando's research (McGuire et al. 1993) on Cerro de Trincheras encompasses the surface survey of the site and two seasons of excavations. Excavations at the site concentrated on possible habitation areas on the northern face of the hill and the western base of the hill, a pit house village south of the main hill, and two ritual areas. A recently completed survey of a 75 square km tract surrounding Cerro de Trincheras has yielded some preliminary observations regarding settlement pattern that can place the intensive research at Cerro de Trincheras in a larger context (Fish 1999). This survey recorded and collected at least 13 cerros de trincheras with total recorded sites numbering more than 240 (Fish 1999:2).

Research on Chihuahuan cerros de trincheras has also witnessed a dramatic increase within the last decade similar to that seen in the Trincheras area. MacWilliams and Kelley (2000) have recently reported on a small cerros de trincheras in west central Chihuahua but a multi-year research project on cerros de trincheras in the Rio Casas Grandes area has had the most dramatic impact on our understanding of cerros de trincheras in Chihuahua and the site type (Roney 1996; Hard and Roney 1998a, 1999).

Cerro Juanaqueña, the most intensively investigated Rio Casas Grandes site, has yielded

Late Archaic C-14 dates (about 1150 B.C.) that considerably extend the temporal span of the site type and suggests that cerros de trincheras originated in this area rather than the Trincheras area. However, our understanding of the site type is continually changing as more research accrues and it is possible that cerros de trincheras in other areas will yield equally early dates. Two other cerros de trincheras in the area date to approximately 1120 B.C. and 100 B.C. (Hard and Roney 1999:28). The data from Cerro Juanaqueña are also transforming our views of the Late Archaic period and early agricultural villages in general. Labor estimates for the 486 terraces at the massive site and the presence of large communal features indicate a higher degree of sedentism and aggregation than archaeologists typically associate with this time period (Hard and Roney 1998b, 1999:29-30; Hard et al. 1999).

Terraces on these Late Archaic sites are constructed by piling rocks to create a crescent shaped berm and they do not have the more formal terrace walls seen on other cerros de trincheras, including Cerro de Trincheras. This technique has recently been observed on an Early Pithouse period site in the Mogollon area (Roney 1999). This is the first recorded example of a cerros de trincheras within this culture area and other undocumented sites may exist (Roney 1999).

Rio Sonoran cerros de trincheras are the least well documented within the culture areas traditionally associated with the site type (Pailes 1972, 1978). The current increase in research on cerros de trincheras in Mexico has largely by-passed the Rio Sonora area, although Doolittle (1988:33-34) has discussed six sites that he interprets as defensive works and possibly signaling stations.

Research on cerros de trincheras in the Hohokam area first documented intensive residential use of these sites, a theme that is echoed in other contemporary investigations. Ironically, Hohokam cerros de trincheras also formed the basis of Wilcox's (1979, 1989) defensive refuge interpretation. While this interpretation did not break any major new ground, it is the most sophisticated and detailed presentation of the defensive refuge position (Wilcox 1979:28-34, 1989).

Wilcox's (1979, 1989) perspective on the site type was originally shaped by his work at Tumamoc Hill in the Tucson Basin (Wilcox and Larson 1979:1-14). In the conclusion to his examination of the defensive aspects of the site, Wilcox (1979:28-34) argued that cerros de trincheras were a defensive reaction to warfare resulting from the tributary demands and competitions of Hohokam chiefdoms. This situation began about A.D. 1100 and lasted until a major reorganization of Hohokam warfare in A.D. 1300, at which point cerros de trincheras were no longer needed. His succeeding interpretation focuses on the collapse of an interaction sphere integrated by shared ideology, elite interaction, and warfare about A.D. 1075-1100. The resulting large-scale instability is evidenced in the construction of fortified sites, including cerros de trincheras. This collapse is followed by a period of political reorganization with integration along major hydrographic zones at A.D. 1250-1300 and alliance formation and competition between elites within these zones that served only to escalate warfare (Wilcox 1989).

The Tumamoc Hill site that inspired these models is now thought to date primarily to A.D. 300-600 (Paul Fish personal communication, 1999) based on material culture. The revised dating for the site invalidates its role in any later conflicts that might have existed and requires readjustment in explanations of cerros de trincheras and warfare in this area.

Other research on Tucson Basin cerros de trincheras has presented a serious challenge to defensive interpretations. Survey and excavations at Linda Vista Hill have renewed active speculation regarding the agricultural uses of terraces and proved that some of the terraces were used for habitation (Fish et al. 1984:11-12; Downum 1986). Agricultural use of terraces is evidenced by pollen samples containing corn from these contexts and agave knifes that may indicate that this plant was grown on terraces (Fish et al. 1984:12). This research has been most useful in disproving the defensive refuge hypothesis, because it produced clear evidence of pit house constructions on terraces. A classic period date has been assigned to this site on the basis of a C-14 sample and associated artifacts (Downum 1986).

Linda Vista Hill appears to have been a residential village, a finding mirrored at another Tucson Basin site, Cerro Prieto, which has approximately 232 masonry residential structures (Downum 1993). The intensive research at Linda Vista Hill and Cerro Prieto has also yielded one of the most comprehensive views of site structure. Both have features comprised of a combination of natural and modified elements that bisect the sites and their proposed residential units, which may reflect a moiety organization (Downum 1993). At Linda Vista Hill, these residential units tend to occur in clusters of 2-13 structures, with exterior activity areas on terraces (Downum 1986:15). Cerro Prieto also had compounds consisting of a stone wall enclosing one or more stone structures, which may have served as community ceremonial spaces (Downum 1993:74-79).

SUMMARY

Organizing a research summary around the concept of "blank" space initially seems to be an odd endeavor. After all, it is research that fills in archaeological unknowns, deletes our "blank" spaces. However, this research must focus on understanding local sequences of development or it is of little utility. Caught up as it was in larger debates regarding its links to the Hohokam, the Trincheras Tradition has not received the attention it has deserved. Ironically, it has also not received the attention necessary to answer the questions formulated in these larger debates. That some of these questions were answered from information gained by the expansive surveys and limited test pit excavations that were the staple of research on the Trincheras Tradition says more about prevailing archaeological mind sets than the reality of the answers. Our understanding of site locations and types and artifact categories was enriched by this research but there are enormous gaps, particularly in the area of chronology, that should not remain after nearly sixty years of research on an archaeological culture. As research in the area moves forward, taking some of the useful theoretical and substantive insights from the past, we have to seek not only to fill in the substantive gaps, but also to challenge broad scale models and theories that ignore local history and process.

Chapter Three
Cerro de Trincheras

The monumental scale and general structure of Cerro de Trincheras are difficult to grasp from written descriptions. Basic information on physical geography and the types, location, and quantity of features cannot truly capture the appearance of the site (Figure 3.1). To fully appreciate the prominence of the site within the surrounding landscape and how the architecture complements and accentuates the topography of the hill, Cerro de Trincheras has to be experienced. I would like to make some attempt at evoking an experiential appreciation of the site in a written format through the medium of a site tour. Standard descriptions of the environment, physiography, and site disturbance are available following the tour.

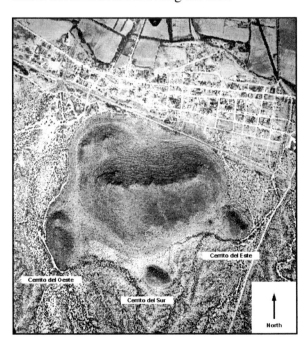

Figure 3.1   Aerial of Cerro de Trincheras by Cooper Aerial. Courtesy of Randall H. McGuire.

Our tour officially begins at the turn onto the Trincheras Road from Mexican Federal Highway 2. The Trincheras Road runs approximately 22 km south from its intersection with Highway 2 to the modern day Pueblo of Trincheras. Cerro de Trincheras is only visible for a short distance approaching from the east along Route 2, since it is obscured by a series of block faulted mountains. The view is clear after the turn onto the Trincheras Road and we can discern Cerro de Trincheras on the southern horizon. Stark in its isolation, a large, dark hill ascends from the river valley, dominating the surrounding landscape. At this distance, Cerro de Trincheras appears in outline and we can only see the undulating curves of the peaks and saddles of its crest and its sloping sides.

The hill looms larger with every passing minute as our tour van transverses the distance to Trincheras. There seems to be little else of interest to look at in this desert landscape. We are passing through an endless and uniform sea of creosote and cholla broken only occasionally by other desert plants and relieved only by the outlines of surrounding hills and mountain ranges.

We have traveled roughly 12 km along the Trincheras Road when we pass a small, nearly invisible turnoff to the west. The dirt track leads to the massive site of La Playa, which stretches to the base of the Boquilla Mountains. The Rio Busani exits these mountains near the site and spreads out onto the plain, severely eroding La Playa in the process. A modern irrigation canal also bisects the site.

Continuing on the bumpy, dusty road, we have finally reached the bed of the Rio Magdalena, a mostly dry channel that currently contains only a trickle of water. The Pueblo of Trincheras stands on the other side of the riverbed. Trincheras is a dusty, depressed railroad town dwarfed by the dark presence that seems to loom over it. The hints of dark bands circling the hill seen from a distance are now clearly discernable as terraces of volcanic rock. From here the terraces appear to stretch in one continuous line across the north face of the site from top to bottom and their step-like progression does give the site some resemblance to pyramids found much farther south (Figure 3.2).

The van makes it way through the pueblo to the base of the north face of the hill and the main gate. This gate leads to a trail to the shrine for the Virgin of Guadalupe and provides the most accessible approach to the site. As we enter, our heads swivel to take in the endless expanse of vegetation and dark rock on the hill. The cerro, an incredibly impressive site at a distance, seems almost overwhelming up close. The view up and along its north face is both breathtaking and oppressive. Terraces ascend all the way to the highest peak. A feeling of insignificance creeps over our group in the face of this huge achievement. The prehistoric inhabitants moved a massive

Figure 3.2   North face of Cerro de Trincheras from the Pueblo of Trincheras, looking southeast. Courtesy of Randall H. McGuire.

amount of rock and soil, carefully stacking and placing it to accent and augment the natural features of this commanding hill.

The trail to the shrine ascends a series of terraces (see Figure 3.3 for a detailed map of the tour route). Some of the rocks that outline the trail could have been mined from the terraces that it winds through. Terraces here are low, barely 40 cm high, and they are really just large lines of rock. They are an inauspicious start to our journey but they provide incentive to continue the ascent towards the larger, more impressive terraces we can see above us.

As we reach the last terrace on the trail, we head westward along the terrace platform, following its masonry retaining wall. There are distinct breaks as we journey forward where the terrace wall curves into the hill. Instead of a continuous line of rock wall extending horizontally along a particular elevation, the terraces are actually a series of adjacent structures. Some have relatively small, low walled, circular structures of rock built into their walls. At the third of these terraces we hit a small trail segment. The path runs through and around a few terraces and then ascends the west side of a low ridge to a wall that runs perpendicular to the hill contour, a prehistoric traffic stop. Here, the trail segment fades out and we decide to head south over the wall to a series of terraces that lead up to La Explanada, the western ridge below the three site peaks. The terraces keep getting higher and are now close to 1 m high. With the increase in elevation the terraces have also become more substantially built and have actual coursed walls in contrast to those at low elevations which were composed of linear piles of rock (Figures 3.4-3.6). The increased height and loose rock make climbing over the terraces difficult.

We have arrived at La Explanada, which is directly below the highest peak, the Buzzard's Roost, or El Pico de Zopilotes. This peak derives its name from these aviators and the debris they

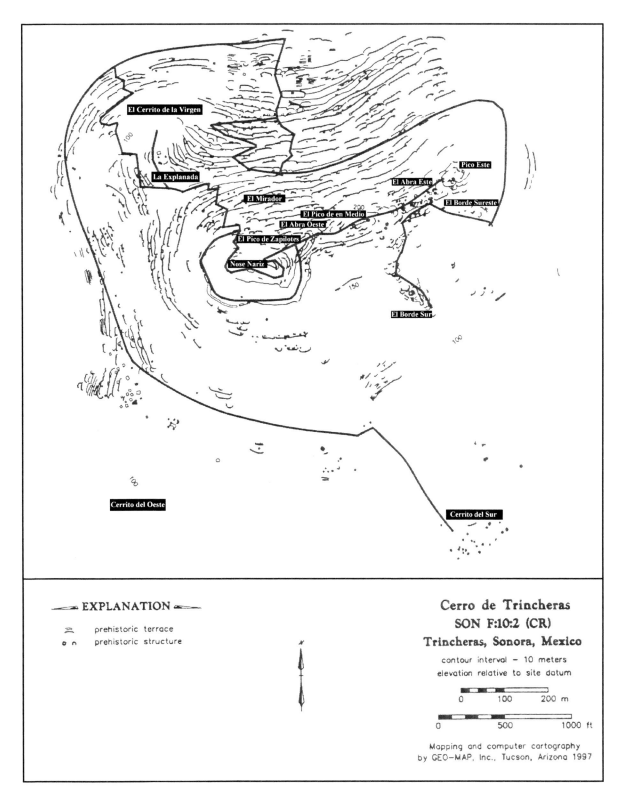

Figure 3.3   Site tour route. Illustration by Mary Lou Supa.

Figure 3.4   Terraces 241,242, and 243 below La Explanada, looking southeast. Courtesy of Randall H. McGuire.

Figure 3.5   Terrace wall and platform at higher elevations of Cerro de Trincheras. Courtesy of Randall H. McGuire.

leave behind. We have still only climbed about 65 m in elevation but some of our party needs to rest. La Explanada is broad and relatively flat, a welcome relief to the steep character of our climb across the terraced hillside. It is a good place to regroup and look around before ascending further.

La Explanada measures approximately 50 m across and it is a little more than twice as long as it is wide, stretching for about 125 m. Areas of bedrock are visible along the ridge and there is little soil deposition here. Some of the bedrock has small, smooth, basin-shaped depressions, fodder for a debate among the tour group regarding whether their origins are natural or cultural. There are few other significant signs of life on La Explanada. Architectural features include only two adjoining circular stone structures and a larger, quadrangular stone structure at the base of a peak, El Cerrito de la Virgen, at the western end of the ridge. Petroglyphs appear on the top of El Cerrito de la Virgen, perhaps marking a trail that begins here leading down to terraces below the southwestern side of La Explanada that doubles back up. The current residents of Trincheras Pueblo have placed a large, white cross at the apex of El Cerrito de la Virgen.

Looking to the north of La Explanada the Pueblo of Trincheras (Figure 3.7) is visible, framed by its canal irrigated fields. The area below us on

Figure 3.6   Front of terrace wall at higher elevations of Cerro de Trincheras. Courtesy of Randall H. McGuire.

the north face contains innumerable terraces that seem to nestle in the natural curve formed by the northern projection of La Explanada. The many terraces in this area have fairly substantial walls (Figure 3.8).

We begin the ascent to El Pico de Zopilotes along the northwestern face, ignoring the terraces that extend up from La Explanada on the western side of the peak due to their sharp inclines. After climbing nearly 100 m in distance and 50 m in elevation we come to a terrace that has a ramp. The ramp is a rock feature in front of the terrace. At this point another trail segment leads up to the peak. The trail splits at the next terrace and part of our party decides to follow the western leg of this trail. As we continue on what appears to be the main trail, we find ourselves passing in front of, and through, a progression of quite short terraces that wind upward through a small gap in the cliff face. Several of these terraces appear to be made entirely of rock. Terraces below this area have dirt platforms behind their rock walls—much more suitable as a living surface.

The main leg of the trail finally leads around a sharp projection of the peak and up onto a very long terrace. The petroglyph at the entrance to this terrace seems to mark the transition to the terraced heights of El Pico de Zopilotes. The prehistoric inhabitants might have considered the trail transitional space from the dirt platform terraces

below that seem to be more practical locations for domestic life to this high, rocky place. The trail leads up along the western side of the peak and then detours directly east to the long terrace on which we are now standing, placing us on the back, or south, side of the hill. The long terrace is one of a series that follow the contours of the triangular shaped portion of the peak along its gentler, southern and western sides. Smaller subsidiary hills to the west, Cerrito del Oeste, and south, Cerrito del Sur (Figure 3.9), are visible.

Noises, some distinct, others murmurs on the wind, have drifted up the hill from the direction of the pueblo since we started ascending it. The crescent shape of the hill seems to pick up sound and amplify it. Now we hear voices coming from be-

Figure 3.8   North face of Cerro de Trincheras showing the heavy terracing here, looking southeast. Courtesy of Randall H. McGuire.

Figure 3.7   Pueblo of Trincheras from Cerro de Trincheras, looking north. Courtesy of Randall H. McGuire.

Figure 3.9   Cerrito del Sur and the southern plain, looking southwest. Courtesy of Randall H. McGuire.

low us on the backside of the hill and assume they belong to the rest of our group. Following the long terrace as it circles around El Pico de Zopilotes to its southeast face, our group looks for an easy place to ascend to the top. The petroglyph at the entrance of the terrace seems to be symbolic of our entrance into an exceptional area, a note to those who came that this was a place of special meaning. With our hopes of spectacular and unusual finds raised, the party starts the ascent to the top in a state of excitement.

We only have another 10 m in distance and elevation to reach the top of the peak. We are disappointed for at the top there is only another substantial terrace flowing along the highest contour of the hill and another petroglyph at its apex. The view from this high point is some compensation. The mountain ranges that encompass the area are visible. Stretching before the southern range to the base of the cerro is a plain deeply cut by arroyos and containing a fairly dense concentration of saguaro.

Another group of terraces guides our descent down the eastern side of El Pico de Zopilotes to the saddle below, El Abra Oeste. The rest of the party awaits us there. The other leg of the trail to El Pico de Zopilotes leads to another long terrace below the peak. From here, they ascended to El Abra Oeste (Figure 3.3) using the terraces as a guide and noticed several of the circular and quadrangular stone structures on terraces along their path. El Abra Oeste is sandwiched between El Pico de Zopilotes and the middle peak, El Pico de en Medio. It is framed from the edge of El Pico de Zopilotes to the base of El Pico de en Medio by a long series of terraces that curve to hug its contours. One terrace has a series of three circular structures. The main portion of the saddle is devoid of architecture and the terraces ringing El Abra Oeste are essentially enclosing, or bracketing, an empty space.

The top of El Pico de en Medio (Figure 3.3) is a relatively short distance and the climb up its

west slope is less precipitous than that up to El Pico de Zopilotes. Scattered terraces occur but we see very few artifacts. In fact, we have not seen many artifacts since leaving the lower elevations of the north face. Due to previous occurrences, the group now associates petroglyphs with peaks and high places and we had expected some here. Unfortunately, the anticipated petroglyphs are absent and, there is only one terrace near the top of El Pico de en Medio. Below us on the south face of the main hill we can make out some outlines of terraces, distinguished by vegetation. Another subsidiary hill is also visible to our east, Cerrito del Este. The subsidiary hills measure slightly more than a third of the height of Cerro de Trincheras, and are certainly insignificant dots in comparison to the overall area of the main hill, but they form an interesting half-ring around it. They lie several hundred meters away from the main hill on all cardinal directions except the north.

The architecture on the eastern side of El Pico de en Medio, descending to the last saddle, El Abra Este, is sparse but varied Figure 3.3). Two of the smaller low terraces, barely 10 m long, occur near the base of the peak. Their diminutive size contrasts with the grandeur of the setting at the exalted heights of the site. But below them is a terrace that is split in half by a more substantial version of one of the circular stone structures and a second terrace with three of the larger, more substantial circular structures. The second terrace does not have the usual crescent shape with ends curving into the hill but has been squared off at each end. It is fairly large and its platform is quite expansive in comparison to others.

Glimpses of El Abra Este from the height of El Pico de en Medio have revealed a number of isolated circular stone structures and terraces arranged across its broad expanse. The eye is immediately drawn to one of these circular stone structures that is considerably larger than the rest with another lower, almost box-like structure attached to its southern side. It sits in relative isolation in a prominent position within the saddle. The architectural arrangement and large number of isolated circular structures, as well as this special structure, seem to indicate that El Abra Este was a unique area.

After visiting innumerable terraces and small structures, our group is eager to investigate El Abra Este, particularly the special structure, El Caracol (Figure 3.10). At first glance the feature appears to be just a scaled up version of one of the circular structures. Its walls, made of dry laid masonry like the terraces, are still standing to a height of almost 1.5 m. Circling around to the south side, we encounter the smaller, attached feature and the entrance to the structure. The wall that forms the east side of the entrance actually folds into the interior to form a spiral shape. The view from the terraces above afforded only a partial glimpse into the interior of El Caracol behind its high walls and we could not see this unique aspect of its design. El Caracol is a rather barren place inside with no artifacts on the surface or architectural embellishment of the interior. The prehistoric inhabitants seem to have formed special places by embellishing barren, natural contexts, adding only more of the rock that is already so ubiquitous on the site. Exploring the rest of El Abra Este, we discover that it is ringed by terraces along its southern side, enclosing it somewhat, although not to the degree of El Abra Oeste. Most of the terraces have been squared off at the ends, demarcating them as separate units in a way that terraces below the crest are not. The north side of El Abra Este has not been as consciously ringed in and we can only see a few, typical terraces below the crest that may have represented some type of barrier. The circular stone structures on this saddle are definitely of a more massive character and have higher, more distinct walls (Figure 3.11). Several of the terraces have these circular stone structures. We have also stumbled upon a unique feature that seems to be a capital letter A made of rocks. This may be a sign of modern disturbance. A large shaft sunk into the hill on the side of the eastern peak, Pico Este, definitely indicates a modern presence. Pico Este affords a good view of an adjacent small, cone shaped hill with several long scars running from its midpoint to its base (a cerros de trincheras named Trincheritas), another oddity in this land of awesome heights and unusual features.

We have barely explored the northern and southern faces of the hill. The northern face is densely terraced but from the crest our glimpses of the southern face seem to indicate that it is not quite as elaborate. The upper regions of the south side are more accessible from the crest and it would be prudent to explore them before moving on to the north face.

After descending to a large terrace directly below the crest, we hit another trail that leads southwestward to a small projection, El Borde Sur (Figure 3.3). There is a small group of terraces here and directly below there is another group strung along a larger extension of El Borde Sur.

Figure 3.10   El Caracol. Courtesy of Randall H. McGuire.

Figure 3.11   Circular stone structure on crest. Courtesy of Randall H. McGuire.

This group surrounds another of the larger circular structures, which seems to form a focal point for the terrace group.

Except for this somewhat unusual cluster of terraces on El Borde Sur, exploring this area seems to offer little potential. Detours in all directions have failed to produce evidence of anything but loose rock. Several trails seem to start at the crest and our group returns here to pick up another, assuming that the trails offer the most direct routes to significant places.

There is a trail starting at El Abra Este that heads down the hill in a southeasterly direction. It offers only scenic vistas, although at one point we think we see a few small terraces off to the east. The trail ends abruptly at the edge of a modest projection, El Borde Sureste, and we are left with no choice but to pick our way around the east side of the hill to reach the north face.

The east side of the hill has nothing except jumbled, loose rock and nasty brush, things found in abundance on this site. An area of steep, rugged terrain forces us to drop to a lower elevation and may have influenced the amount of architecture here. A short distance later, we finally emerge onto a terrace. As we proceed across the north face of the hill following the terraces a glance up reveals that we are below El Abra Este. A bit farther along we hit a continuous line of terraces at the same elevation. Two of these terraces have smaller terraces directly above them. The smaller terraces lie between this and the next line of terraces and break up the vertical flow of architecture. These terraces have quite steep sides and at 11 m long are about half the length of the surrounding terraces.

The number of stone tools and pottery appears to have increased as we have headed westward along this line of terraces. The density of the artifacts indicates that we are in an area filled with the debris of daily life, which contrasts sharply with the hill crest where artifacts are relatively scarce.

The line of terraces ends abruptly near El Pico de Zopilotes. Exploring more of the terraces along the north face does not appeal to most of the group. The sheer number of terraces and the repetitious pattern is numbing. With the exception of the smaller terraces located between terrace lines, most of the terraces vary little. They all have the substantial walls characteristic of the high reaches of the site and their length or width changes only slightly. The terraces seem to offer few opportunities for new discoveries, so we decide to continue our tour elsewhere.

The prehistoric occupants may have built on the level ground surrounding the hill and this area may offer new things to see. The group fans out to the east and west to explore more of the site as we descend. Discoveries may still await us on the northern face. The number of circular stone structures seems to increase to the west in the area below La Explanada. Many of the terraces have several circular features, contrasting with the pattern of one, or none, that we have noticed in other areas. Someone has even spotted a painted potsherd here.

The eastern side of our group has also seen a very wide terrace directly below them. As the group converges on this feature, La Cancha, everyone heaves a sigh of relief at reaching more level terrain. La Cancha (Figure 3.12) is indeed very broad, more than triple the width of the average terrace and it has partially enclosed ends. As we explore this feature, we realize that it is more like some type of earthen platform sandwiched between the terraces. There is a circular structure about midway along the platform against the down slope wall. La Cancha seems to be yet another special area, although it is not demarcated in any significant way as the crest was.

Renewing our goal of reaching the fence line surrounding the site, we skirt around the western edge of La Cancha and come into an open area devoid of rock works. As our party continues down in a westerly direction, we hit a series of very closely spaced low, narrow terraces (Figure 3.13) and then the fence line. Heading west along the fence line, we finally encounter a dirt track, the other branch of the road into the site.

The road climbs up a short, sharp incline and passes around a small projection to the west of La Explanada. Walking along its now mercifully level course, we spot scattered groups of terraces below us that extend up the main hill. After walking perhaps 600 to 700 m, our party sees a large, low, square rock outline near the western subsidiary hill, Cerrito del Oeste. It is surrounded by several smaller square rock outlines. Terraces occur downslope from this area.

Following the road once more we take a detour that heads to Cerrito del Sur (Figure 3.3). Walking around near the base of this hill we encounter one terrace, a few rock rings, some potsherds, and stone tools. The rings are lower and

Figure 3.12   Western end of La Cancha. Courtesy of Randall H. McGuire.

Figure 3.13   Narrow terraces below La Cancha. Courtesy of Randall H. McGuire.

less substantial than the circular stone structures, which generally have more than one course of masonry. There are also several recent holes with backdirt still scattered around them.

The light is beginning to fade and our party has agreed to head back to the van. Extending our visit to see the eastern hill is probably not worth the aggravation of late night driving and most of us are exhausted. As we head back to the van along the dirt road, some of our party continue to speculate on how the site was used: Was it an ancient fort? Or did people actually prefer to live on a hillside for some other reason? At the van, we all pile in, grateful for the cushioned seats and the chance to get off our feet. It has been a long and tiring day but it was worth the effort to see this spectacular, ancient ruin.

This imaginative scenario conveys how modern visitors might experience Cerro de Trincheras—a fascinating, somewhat inexplicable, and formidable ruin towering over a dry, dusty plain. Changes in the landscape and site wrought by recent history would not be readily apparent to these tourists, with the exception of looter's holes, and many of these changes are still not fully understood by archaeologists.

ENVIRONMENT

Cerro de Trincheras lies in the heart of the Sonoran Desert, known for its biannual pattern of rainfall. The area receives both winter precipitation along large fronts originating in the Pacific Ocean and monsoons, strong summer rainstorms from the Gulf of Mexico (MacMahon 1985:28, 62). Summer precipitation is less advantageous for vegetation growth and moisture retention, because its rapid rate erodes the ground more than it saturates. Precipitation and temperature vary by elevation with higher elevations receiving more precipitation and having lower temperatures. This pattern has a profound effect on vegetation cover.

The Rio Magdalena Valley falls in the Lower Colorado Valley vegetation subdivision of the Sonoran Desert. Creosote and white bursage are the two dominant plant species and can comprise up to 90 percent of the plant life in plain areas. Cholla is also found on the plains and dense colonies can occur in areas grazed by cattle that spread the bud segments. Run-off channels along the valley floors create pockets of higher effective moisture, increasing species diversity. Diversity also increases in the lower bajada areas above the valley floors where small trees and various species of cacti thrive. The most common trees are the foothill paloverde and mesquite. Ocotillo, a multi-stemmed succulent, also occurs here. The upper bajada areas are home to the cacti, most notably the columnar varieties, including saguaro, cardon, and organ pipe. Agave also does well in these areas but is not a common plant. Several species of cholla grow throughout the bajada region (MacMahon 1985:64-65).

This environmental context provides opportunities for gathering wild plant foods, primarily in the bajada areas, and sets limits for agricultural productivity. The cacti were the major resources exploited by ethnohistoric populations in the area, although a variety of other wild plants were used (Russell 1975:69-80). The fruit of the saguaro cactus and cholla buds were harvested and roasted (Underhill 1939:98). Agricultural limitations in this desert environment stem primarily from the availability of water. Rainfall in the region averages slightly less than 300 mm annually, which is not adequate for agriculture without an additional water source (Fish 1999:4). Floodplains of the major river valleys were ideal areas for agriculture and prehistoric populations could have cultivated corn in adjacent areas using both ground water and irrigation technology. Some of the larger, expansive washes also could have supported floodwater fields.

We currently have little information on prehistoric environmental conditions in the Cerro de Trincheras area. Appraisals based on modern data are always problematic but the distribution of economically useful plant species in the bajada areas is probably similar to prehistoric conditions, since these areas were not settled and modified to the extent that floodplain areas were. Cerro de Trincheras is located in a prime spot to take advantage of both the agricultural potential of the floodplain and the wild resources in the floodplain and bajada areas. The site lies between the floodplain of the Rio Magdalena and the large bajada area that spreads out from the Sierra Santa Rosa, some 20 km distant. Multitudes of small washes and arroyos cut this bajada. They are filled with mesquite, providing an abundant supply of firewood, and saguaro and organ pipe (McGuire et al. 1993:18). The distribution of bajada plant species essentially continues into the immediate site area where it meets the floodplain.

The floodplain of the Rio Magdalena would have been a crucial resource for the agricultural populations living at Cerro de Trincheras. However, today, the Rio Magdalena only flows near Trincheras Pueblo during particularly heavy periods of rain, because its flow is diverted by a dam and canal system located upstream. The modern dam, canal system, and pumping for domestic water use and irrigation have significantly lowered the water table and altered drainage patterns. To get a better idea of the prehistoric conditions, we must turn to sketchy, early accounts of the site.

Manje was the first European to visit and record his impressions of the Trincheras area. His diary for February of 1694 indicates that local conditions were much wetter. There was a lake near the settlement of Ocuca (23 km north of Trincheras) and he called the area surrounding the Rio Magdalena a "vega" (Burrus 1971:291-298). Spanish dictionaries of the period define "vega" as low, wet country (McGuire et al. 1993:18).

This lush landscape receded as cattle began to fill the landscape. By the 1890s overgrazing and other practices that reduced vegetation cover contributed to a major cycle of erosion throughout the Sonoran Desert. The Rio Magdalena, and other major rivers, became entrenched resulting in a lower water table (Sauer and Brand 1931:91-92). We have two accounts by local residents that suggest that the Rio Magdalena spread out and formed a cienega in front of Cerro de Trincheras before this period. Sauer and Brand (1931:92) reported oral accounts by residents of a cienega at Trincheras approximately fifty years prior to their survey. During our survey, a pueblo resident, Gerardo Murrieta, placed this cienega at the base of the hill and called it a small lake. The information came from his mother, who experienced the lake as a child during the late nineteenth century.

Oral tradition supplies no definite date for the entrenchment of the Rio Magdalena. Published accounts and photos from early explorers suggest that the river may have entrenched prior to McGee's 1895 visit to the site and had definitely entrenched by 1910, when Huntington (1914) photographed Trincheras (McGuire et al. 1993:19).

The existence of a cienega at the base of Cerro de Trincheras is an open issue until a definitive reconstruction of the prehistoric environment is completed. Regardless of the outcome of this reconstruction, we can still surmise that the Rio Magdalena was closer to the surface than at present and would have represented an ideal spot for agriculture within this desert landscape. Archaeological evidence for agricultural features near the Rio Magdalena is currently slim. Modern pueblo construction and irrigation canals may have obscured prehistoric agricultural features in many cases. Huntington (1914:69) did describe possible agricultural features on the level ground south of the main hill. The features were rectangular rock outlines measuring approximately 40 by 100 feet (12 by 30 m) that he thought were gridded gardens, indicating that some agricultural production may have occurred outside the main river plain. Whether the terraces were primarily used for ag-

ricultural production, as Huntington (1912, 1914) suggested, is an issue addressed in the site architectural analysis in chapter five.

SITE DISTURBANCE

Cerro de Trincheras continues to hold relevance for townspeople today. Cerro de Trincheras remains part of the town in a very real sense, because it is owned by the *ejido*, or communal land agency, of Trincheras. A shrine to the Virgin of Guadalupe, an image painted on a plastered cliff face, and its associated cross and trail are located on El Cerrito de la Virgen. Community contact with the site also includes less sacred activities. Any ejido member can graze their cattle on the site. Cow trails and crushed artifacts mark the surface. The constant contact has had detrimental impacts. For example, cattle trodding is probably responsible for the relatively small size of artifacts.

However, brief, intense episodes have resulted in the greatest damage to the site. The construction of a railroad during the early 1940s linking Baja California with interior regions of the country had the greatest impact on the site. The rail line sits atop a high berm at the base of the cerro, dividing it from the Pueblo of Trincheras. The volcanic hills surrounding the right-of-way provided the loose cobbles, among other materials, which form much of this berm. Local residents have described crews pushing rock down the hillsides to be loaded into trucks. What was probably a very efficient strategy by railroad engineer standards has proved to be disastrous for some trincheras located on these hills. The long, buff colored scars on Trincheritas, the site directly east of Cerro de Trincheras, have fascinated visitors to the area for years. An examination of Gordon Ekholm's photos from 1937, which are on file at the American Museum of Natural History, clearly indicated that the scars were absent at this time. Stone mining and a loading ramp have disturbed approximately fifty percent of the surface area of Trincheritas.

Cerro de Trincheras fared slightly better than Trincheritas, escaping with only minor damage to some areas. The construction efforts may have obliterated the features Huntington (1914:69) described as gridded gardens near the south base of the cerro. We know that the south side of the hill and Cerrito del Sur were sources of rock for the construction. Several oval piles of rock near Cerrito del Sur are probably related to these activities and some of the square rock outlines which appeared to be stone structures near Cerrito del Oeste may be the spoils of past rock mining expeditions. Other sources of rock for railway construction concentrate to the east, both along the main hill slope and near Cerrito del Este. Most of the intensively occupied north face of the site was spared, although a small portion of its extreme eastern end shows signs of disturbance.

The east end of the cerro has also been the site of other forms of disturbance. Pico Este shows evidence of blasting related to prospecting and a road has been cut up the east side of the hill, presumably to facilitate these operations. Our modern day, fictional tourists found a rock feature resembling the letter A slightly below Pico Este. The origin of this feature initially perplexed us. We learned the tale behind this feature during our stay in the town during the spring of 1995, much to our delight and chagrin. It is not a cattle brand, our best guess; it is not even the letter "A". The feature signifies the Roman numeral five, placed there by elementary school students during a tour of the hill. Excavations at the lower elevations of the northeast side of the cerro have also revealed bulldozer cutting. It appears that the long, slightly off angle terraces in this area are a result of this activity and that La Cancha, the large ritual feature here, was also impacted.

The main cerro shows little evidence of pothunting, with fewer than twenty looter's holes in the terraces on the front face. The exclusive location of El Pico de Zopilotes must have intrigued someone, because the rock-filled terraces on its east slope show evidence of their activities. Other looters hit on a more profitable area. The cremation cemetery located between Cerrito del Sur and the base of the main cerro has been extensively looted. In fact, our interpretation of this area is based on the scattered contents of these holes. An informal artifact pipeline apparently existed between local residents and California buyers interested in pots from this area. The enclosure of the site with a 2 m high fence by INAH in 1990 was aimed at deterring these activities.

A less visible, and therefore less calculable, form of artifact loss comes through casual collecting, which can certainly affect surface artifact distributions. Several people in town have unusual artifacts, or well made utilitarian items, that they have collected from the site surface. Visitors to Cerro de Trincheras may also collect "souvenirs." The almost complete lack of projectile points on the surface may be attributable to casual collecting.

SUMMARY

Our modern tour group gained some appreciation of the general structure of the site. They recognized the special, probably sacred, character of the crest by the unique characteristics of its architecture and arrangement. They were also able to contrast this with other areas that contained more artifacts and soil deposits that may have been domestic areas. This observant group also noticed smaller details, such as differences in terrace and structure types and the signs of disturbance left by modern pothunting and mining activities. Most importantly, they conveyed to us, in an attenuated form, what might be termed the "flow" of the site, how all of the pieces come together or transform from one area to the next. The general structure of the site may be best evoked in the form of a tour that conveys personal experiences rather than dry statistics but these are also an essential component of our understanding of life at Cerro de Trincheras, the subject of the following chapter.

Chapter Four
The Cerro de Trincheras Survey

The principal goals of the Cerro de Trincheras survey were to produce a reliable and accurate map of the site and obtain information on artifact and architectural classes and their surface distributions. The initial problem the project confronted was the efficient production of a map for a site that covered 1 km² and encompassed some 150 m of elevation change. Photometric techniques provided an ideal solution and we were able to map all visible architectural features and complete systematic artifact collections in a seven week field season. Architectural features include two ritual features in addition to the terraces and circular and square stone structures frequently found on cerros de trincheras. These features and the artifact collections are briefly described following the discussion of survey methodology.

METHODOLOGY

Photometric Mapping

We had originally intended to use photometric techniques only for topographic mapping. However, initial examination of the aerial photo proofs revealed that large site features, including many terraces, were clearly visible and that thematic mapping was possible. Several large features could actually be mapped directly from the aerial photo, although all feature positions were ground-truthed by survey crews. Standard photometric techniques were used to accomplish the topographic and thematic mapping. Geo-Map of Tucson handled all phases of the photometric mapping process and continues to be involved in site mapping.

Geo-Map produced a preliminary map prior to the 1991 field season and provided blue line copies of enlargements of the aerial photo for field mapping. Sections of the blue lines were mounted on cardboard and used by survey crews to locate and map archaeological features and artifact sampling units. All survey information was transferred to mylar copies of the aerial with indelible ink for archival purposes.

Distortion inherent in aerial photos is the major disadvantage for mapping. Cerro de Trincheras is not an ideal site for aerial imaging, given that it ascends approximately 150 m out of a surrounding plain. The mapping team attempted to compensate for the distortion produced by site topography while maintaining adequate resolution for mapping by flying the aerials at an optimal altitude of 1450 m above ground level. A survey control network was also established on the site using survey monuments previously set by INAH. This network provided accurate horizontal and vertical coordinates for the photometric mapping process. The site coordinate system is relative. However, if the necessary survey work is completed the coordinates can be tied into the UTM system.

Map distortion was rectified during conversion into digital format. The locations of features identified during topographic and thematic mapping were used for comparison during the rectification process in addition to established survey positions. Displacement of features due to nonlinear distortion of the scale extended to a maximum of 40 m (see McGuire et al. 1993: 13-14).

Production of a final map for the site is a continuing process. Excavations at the site conducted in 1995 and 1996 exposed features, requiring some modifications to the map. Figure 4.1 (CD in jacket) shows the most recent version of the map. The flexibility and efficiency of the mapping system selected has, and will, enable researchers to make changes with relative ease.

Field Survey

The surface survey of Cerro de Trincheras was conducted during the late fall of 1991, following a relatively dry summer. Vegetation was sparse due to the dry conditions, increasing surface visibility, which was generally good across the site. Terraces were chosen as the main units of observation. They are the most numerous architectural class on the site and had been identified as residential areas at other cerros de trincheras (Downum 1986). Field crews plotted, recorded, and made artifact collections from 880 terraces.

All architectural features visible on the surface, including non-terrace features, were located and plotted. This process was made easier by the visibility of many features on the aerial photos used for field mapping. A line of vegetation often indicated terraces and in some cases the actual feature wall was visible. Field crews generally used vegetation patterning to map in features, although in some cases the fence surrounding the site and trails provided additional markers.

We were not able to record all non-terrace features in detail due to time limitations. Two of the non-terrace features, El Caracol and La Cancha, are unique but quadrangular and circular stone structures and rock arrangements number in the tens to hundreds. To compensate for the lack of systematic dimensional and artifact data on the three most numerous non-terrace feature classes, we selected one example of each for detailed recording. This process consisted of making a tape-and-compass map of the feature, photographing it, and collecting artifacts. The two unique non-terrace features were also recorded using this same set of procedures.

From the base of the main hill the terraces seem to comprise a series of very long horizontal lines that extend across the entire north face of the main hill. Early descriptions, many of which were not based on extensive observation, contain estimates of the number of terraces that range from 20 to 100 (Burrus 1971; Lumholtz 1912; Huntington 1914). Systematic examination revealed that the long lines are actually formed by a series of small terraces along the same elevation. We defined terraces as distinct entities for recording purposes based on three criteria: an abrupt change in elevation which separated terrace lines, a wall bisecting the width of the terrace fill platform, and a break in the terrace wall not obviously due to collapse. In most cases terrace breaks were quite distinct, because terrace ends tend to curve into the hillside creating a small gap. However, dense vegetation, wall collapse, and complex prehistoric modifications and expansions often obscured terrace edges or distinctions. The terrace count after two seasons of excavation is now closer to 900 than 880, the 1991 survey total. The increase in the terrace count principally stems from instances where we missed breaks between terraces that became evident once an area was cleared for excavation. We feel that the current figure represents a number close to the total but there still may be instances where we have misinterpreted terrace breaks or areas where we have missed a few terraces.

Detailed recording of each terrace included a standard set of dimensional information and artifact collection and counts. Length, width, and height of terrace wall, width of the terrace fill platform, and type of terrace fill were recorded for all terraces. Terrace fill determinations were based on surface observations and were restricted to rock, gravel, soil, or combinations of these. Dimensional and fill information can be useful in distinguishing habitation terraces. The detailed dimensional data also allowed us to calculate labor estimates for the site, providing a rough comparative index of site scale (see Chapter Six).

The number of points for width and height measurements per terrace was determined by terrace length. Terraces 10 m or less in length had only one set of measurements taken at the midpoint of the terrace. Terraces between 10 m and 30 m long were measured at the mid-point and at each end of the terrace. In cases of terraces over 30 m long, field crews took width and height measurements every 10 m.

The placement of artifact collection and count units on terraces corresponded to the measurement procedures. Field crews made at least one controlled collection of artifacts on each terrace, which was placed at the mid-point on terraces less than 30 m in length. Terraces over 30 m in length had collection units at every third measurement point. We supplemented the collection units with controlled count units at all other measurement points. Artifact counts were broken down by artifact type and noted on the recording forms. Artifact units were either 1 or 2 m diameter circles, with the larger units being used to increase the sample size in cases where artifact densities were extremely low. Crews collected artifacts from 992 units and, in addition to these, artifact counts are available for 1,412 units.

A total collection strategy was employed for rare and time sensitive artifacts. Rare artifacts included non-local sherds and possible high status "luxury" items. Prior to the 1995 and 1996 excavation seasons, there were no absolute dates for Cerro de Trincheras, and only a few, late dates for the Trincheras Tradition that proved more controversial than enlightening. Initial chronological placement of the site had to rely primarily on cross-dated local decorated types and securely dated non-local types. Shell jewelry is the only item commonly found on the site that may be associated with status differences. A comprehensive collection of shell would provide more data to examine important interpretative issues, including consumption and exchange. Non-local pottery types can also be used to infer some aspects of exchange relations. Survey crews systematically walked each terrace and collected all rare artifacts that occurred outside artifact units as a general collection for the terrace. These artifacts were provenienced by terrace number.

We also employed a total documentation strategy for ground stone artifacts to increase the sample size. Most large ground stone artifacts, such as metates, were recorded in the field and left there. Field crews noted type and material information and measured and photographed ground stone that was not collected.

Most prehistoric activity occurred on the main cerro but some architectural features and evidence of specific activities are found at the surrounding base of the hill and near subsidiary hills. The largest concentration of artifacts and features outside the main hill is near Cerrito del Sur, where we found a looted cremation cemetery and several rock arrangements. To examine this subsidiary area, we placed 33 survey transects around and to the northwest of Cerrito del Sur running beyond Cerrito del Oeste (Figures 3.3, 4.1). The transects were spaced 20 m apart as were artifact collection and count units of 1 m diameter. Every third artifact unit was collected and artifact counts were recorded for other units. These artifact units are included in the totals for artifact collection and count units discussed above (see McGuire et al. 1993:14-16 for additional information).

ARCHITECTURAL FEATURES

Researchers have long recognized that Cerro de Trincheras is a unique expression of the site type (Lumholtz 1912; Johnson 1960, 1963; Bowen n.d.). It is the largest known cerros de trincheras but it is not simply a scaled up version of a "typical" cerros de trincheras. The site has the widest variety of architectural features, including two large ritual features. Basic descriptions of the feature classes recorded during the survey that mark Cerro de Trincheras as a unique and important site among its counterparts are given below.

Terraces

Terraces are ubiquitous on the site and at first glance seem to represent a uniform feature class. Terraces are characterized by dry laid masonry walls which are used to retain the flat, fill platforms that dovetail with the hill slope. A terrace typology was constructed and used to classify terraces for recording and analysis (Table 4.1). There is some overlap in dimensional characteristics between the types; therefore, observed differences in wall construction were the primary factors used to determine type assignment in ambiguous cases. Terraces can be divided into three categories: 1) terraces with walls have well defined, masonry walls; 2) terraces have retaining walls that were more loose piles of rock; and 3) narrow terraces are only one masonry course deep.

Differences between these terrace types reflect slope and/or elevation and function. A positive relationship between slope gradient and terrace type is clearly evident in Table 4.1. Terraces with walls only occur above 80 m elevation, the general point at which the average slope gradient more than doubles, increasing from 16% to 34%. The increased quality of, and investment in, terrace wall construction above the 16% average slope gradient is a product of two related requirements. The height of the terrace wall must increase as the vertical angle increases in order to retain the same surface area for the terrace platform. This increased height necessitates more substantial terrace walls, because the increased fill volume exerts more pressure on these walls. Decreased stability on steeper slopes may also influence wall thickness and durability and must have led to more frequent maintenance. Terraces with walls, on steep gradients, are more likely to exhibit collapse than other terraces (see McGuire et al. 1993:23-26).

The relationship between terrace height and average slope gradient is illustrated in Table 4.2, where the hill is divided into three zones of increasing elevation. The most dramatic increase in wall height comes at approximately 80 m elevation, at which point we see corresponding morphological changes in the terraces, which feature substantial retaining walls. The highest average slope gradient, 57%, falls between 125 m and 165 m. The increase in average wall height here is only 41 cm. It seems that once an average slope gradient of 34% is reached, increases in wall height are less dramatic. The 57% average slope gradient is primarily remarkable for containing terraces with the highest walls along the steepest slopes (see McGuire et al. 1993:23-26).

Functional variation within the terrace typology is best illustrated by the contrast between narrow terraces and terraces. Both are found at the lower elevations of the site but narrow terraces are much less substantial. While they average 1.95

Terrace Type	Narrow		Terraces		Terraces/Walls	
	Average	Range	Average	Range	Average	Range
Width	1.95 m	<1.5 m	3.54 m	1.5-5 m	3.5 m	1.5-5 m
Length	10.07 m	<20 m	21.02 m	10->100 m	21.15 m	10->100 m
Height	0.38 m	0.1-0.50 m	0.65 m	>0.3-1.5 m	1.28 m	1.5-3 m
Area	20.27 m		87.5 m		80.44 m	
Elevation	<=80 m		<=80 m		>80 m	
Average Slope Gradient	16%		16%		34-57%	
Total	49		301		530	

Table 4.1 - Terrace Typology

m wide, some measure less than 1.5 m in width and are formed by only a single course of rock. Narrow terraces generally cluster in groups of 10-20 at elevations below 75 m. Most occur below La Cancha, the large platform located at the center of the north face of the main hill. The size and clustering of these terraces indicate that they were restricted to one use, perhaps agriculture, whereas the other two types are large enough to have served a number of purposes.

Field crews recorded surface observations of terrace fill type as this was deemed a possible indicator of variability in use. Most terraces contained soil or earth fill and only 38 terraces with no visible soil were designated as rock filled. It is difficult to image people living on rock filled terraces, but this variable may not be a reliable indicator of prehistoric use. The preponderance of earth or soil fill in terraces says very little about the actual activities that may have occurred on these features. Excavation data have also revealed that our surface determinations may be inaccurate in some cases and some terraces recorded as earth or soil filled are actually primarily filled with trash while others have fill primarily composed of rock. Due to the ambiguities associated with the variable of fill type, it was not used in further analysis.

Walls

Differentiating between a wall and a terrace is something of judgement call but the distinction is relevant, since walls at the site seem to have served only one function. The eight walls recorded during the survey primarily occur at the higher elevations of the main hill and are almost exclusively used to block access, or sight, into portions of this area of the site. We differentiated walls from terraces by the absence of a fill platform connecting the wall to the hill. Walls do not appear to be a common feature on cerros de trincheras but they have been reported from several sites in Arizona and Sonora (Ives 1936; Stacy 1974; McGuire and Villalpando 1993; Wilcox 1979; see also McGuire et al. 1993:26).

Circular Stone Structures

Circular stone structures are a frequent occurrence on cerros de trincheras (Lumholtz 1912; Fontana et al. 1959; Johnson 1963; Hoover 1941; Fraps 1936; Stacy 1974; Wilcox 1979) and can include large summit features and smaller structures often associated with terraces. The term corral has been applied to both summit features, which probably played a limited, perhaps ritual, role involving community organization (Fish 1999), and the more ubiquitous smaller structures (Lumholtz 1912:9; Hinton 1955:5). Smaller structures have been interpreted as sleeping circles (Fontana et al. 1959) but recent research indicates that at least some may define domestic contexts (Downum 1986; Downum et al. 1994). The catchall nature of the term corral, and its implications, make it a poor choice to describe any features. We prefer to use basic descriptive terms that avoid any previous connotations and acknowledge the morphological differences between summit features and the larger class of circular stone structures (McGuire et al. 1993:27).

Circular stone structures are the second most numerous architectural feature at Cerro de Trincheras. Of the 271 circular stone structures recorded during the survey, 236 are associated with terraces (Figure 4.2) while the remaining 35 are isolated examples (Figure 4.3). The isolated examples tend to occur on the crest of the hill and are generally larger than those associated with terraces. One forms the focal point for a group of

Table 4.2 - Terrace Wall Height and Slope Gradient

Elevation	Average Slope	Average Wall Height
<=80 m	16%	0.43 m
>80, <=125 m	34%	1.04 m
>125, <=165 m	57%	1.45 m

Note: Terraces at the crest of the site, which varies in slope gradient with the topography of peaks and saddles, are not included in this table.

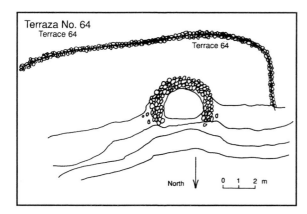

Figure 4.2   Plan of terrace 64 showing circular stone structure. Drafted by Anne Hull. Courtesy of Randall H. McGuire.

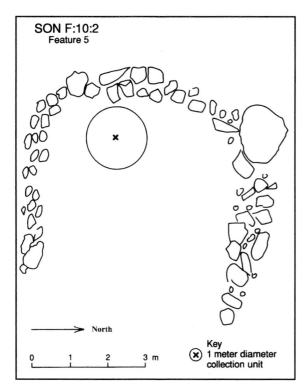

Figure 4.3   Plan of feature 5, a circular stone structure. Drafted by Anne Hull. Courtesy of Randall H. McGuire.

terraces on El Borde de Sur. We do not have systematic information for circular stone structures but survey crews made a few observations on the general characteristics. The structures range in diameter from approximately 1.5 to 5.0 m and have walls to 1 m high. However, most of the structures outside the hill crest are closer to 1.5 to 2.0 m in diameter. Circular stone structures are composed of dry laid masonry walls. Some of these features sit directly on bedrock and many have few, or no, artifacts within their boundaries (see McGuire et al. 1993:27-32).

Quadrangular Stone Structures

Quadrangular stone structures are primarily distinguished from circular stone structures by their shape. We plotted 57 of these features during the survey and they also occur as isolates and in association with terraces. Quadrangular stone structures may represent variations of circular stone structures. Again, this feature class was not systematically measured and artifacts were not collected. These features range from approximately 3 to 5 m wide and 4 to 6 m long (McGuire et al. 1993:32). As with the circular structures, the isolated examples are generally much larger than those associated with terraces. Most of the 22 isolated structures occur near Cerrito del Oeste, although a few scattered structures occur on or near the crest and at the lower elevations of the main hill.

Excavation of quadrangular stone structures near Cerrito del Oeste during the 1995 season revealed a potential problem with our surface determinations in this area. For example, the largest of these features consisted of a single level of rocks and appears to be a result of modern disturbance. The southern and western sides of the site were robbed of rock that was used in the construction of the berm for the rail line that runs in front of the site. Therefore, this large feature may be the result of temporary rock piling for construction. Not all of our initial classifications were incorrect, however, as at least one of the quadrangular stone structures was identified as a prehistoric room. Distinguishing between these two types of square features based on surface evidence is difficult and we now believe that only half, or fewer, of the square features in this cluster are actual prehistoric structures.

Trails

Prehistoric trails have been recorded at several cerros de trincheras sites (Fontana et al. 1959; Stacy 1974; McGuire and Villalpando 1993; Wilcox 1979; Downum 1993). Given its size and variability, our expectation is that Cerro de Trincheras had an extensive prehistoric trail system. During the survey we found segments of several trails but could only follow lengthy segments of two trails.

The two trails are located on the western and eastern sides of the main cerro and ascend to its crest (Figure 4.1). Extant segments that field crews could trace measure over 100 m. Discernable traces of the eastern trail begin at about 150 m in elevation at which point the trail ascends to El Abra Este. The eastern side of the hill is highly disturbed and this may have obliterated evidence of the trail at lower elevations. Traces of the western trail begin on the north face near El Pico de Zopilotes. From there the trail winds through a gap in the sheer northern cliff face of El Pico de Zopilotes and emerges on its south side. Several very short trail segments occur to the west, directly below El Pico de Zopilotes, and to the northwest, ascending into La Explanada. These segments may have formed part of a larger system that funneled traffic from several different areas of the site to the crest.

Terraces seem to have been used to regulate movement on both trails. Trail terraces support switchbacks that would have made the ascent easier and also serve to guide traffic along a defined course that could be easily controlled. Some terraces along the trails had either wall openings or ramps that directed movement. Terraces with wall breaks and ramps also occur in other areas

of the site including places of high terrace density. It is possible that the terraces themselves formed the primary pathways through the site (McGuire et al. 1993:26).

Rock Arrangements

Rock arrangements only occur south of Cerrito del Sur and are associated with a known pit house village. The features are oval to circular rings of stone, generally 3-4 m in diameter (Figure 4.4). We mapped 25 of these features during the survey but their distribution extended beyond the boundaries of the site map and there may be another two dozen, or so, of these structures left unplotted (McGuire et al. 1993:27). Excavations in the spring of 1995 confirmed that some of these rock rings outline pit house structures (McGuire 1997). The current suite of C-14 dates from the

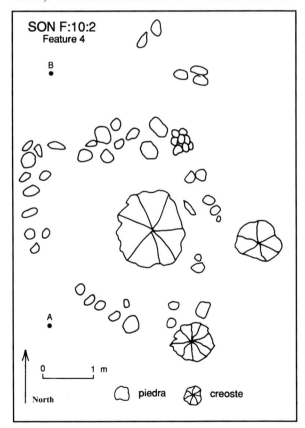

Figure 4.4   Plan of feature 4, a rock arrangement. Drafted by Anne Hull. Courtesy of Randall H. McGuire.

site indicate that the pit house village is probably contemporaneous with the main hill occupation (McGuire 1997).

La Cancha

McGee (2000 [1895]:62) first noted this feature but Huntington (1914:68), who termed it a "ceremonial platform," provided the best description. This large feature is clearly evident on Huntington's (1914:plate 2c) early photo of the site and on our aerial photos.

La Cancha lies near the base of the hill on its north face, roughly at its center. It is sandwiched between terrace levels and is morphologically distinct from the surrounding terraces. The earthen fill of the La Cancha platform measures approximately 11 m wide; including the walls, it is approximately 15 m. La Cancha is 57 m long and its end walls are rounded. Small breaks occur in both end walls of the structure, the eastern one opening onto terrace 607. A circular stone structure measuring 2.7 m in diameter is located at approximately the midpoint of the northern, or downslope, wall of La Cancha (Figures 4.5 and 4.6; McGuire et al. 1993:33-35).

Excavation of the feature during the spring of 1996 disclosed bulldozer cuts. These correspond to the breaks in the western and eastern sides of the feature and La Cancha may have originally been fully enclosed. A line of rocks visible on the surface running from the circular stone structure to the break in the western side also appears to stem from bulldozer activities (McGuire and Villalpando 2000).

Detailed references to similar features in the literature are relatively rare. McGuire (1985:12) recorded a large rectangular feature measuring 12 by 37 m at Son:F:11:5, a hill west of Caborca, and Braniff (1985) has excavated a test pit in a rectangular feature measuring 17.2 by 32.3 m at La Calera. Test excavations at La Calera located a floor level but provided little other information.

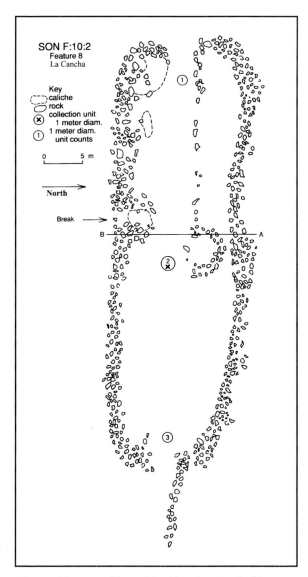

Figure 4.5   Plan of La Cancha. Drafted by Anne Hull. Courtesy of Randall H. McGuire.

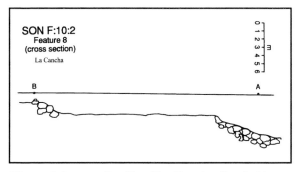

Figure 4.6   Profile of La Cancha. Drafted by Anne Hull. Courtesy of Randall H. McGuire.

El Caracol

El Caracol has been commented on by many visitors to the site (McGee 2000[1895]; Lumholtz 1912; Huntington 1914; Ekholm 1937). It is a spiral shaped feature (Figure 4.7) located in a prominent position within El Abra de Este. The location of El Caracol and its unique shape suggest that it was an important, specialized structure.

The dry laid masonry walls of El Caracol still stand to a maximum height of approximately 1.5 m and the low amount of rubble around the base of the structure indicates that the walls were not originally much higher. The primary feature has a maximum length of 12.6 m and a maximum width of 7.7 m. The sub-structure attached to the exterior of the feature on its south wall is oval in plan view, with walls ranging from 70 cm to 87 cm high, and measures 4.5 by 4 m (McGuire et al. 1993:35-38).

Large summit features are one of the defining characteristics of cerros de trincheras (Lumholtz 1912:9; Hinton 1955:5; McGuire and Villalpando 1993:66; Stacy 1974; Kirk 1994). Hinton (1955:5) describes summit features in the Altar Valley as largely square in outline and measuring up to 60 by 60 feet (18.3 by 18.3 m). To my knowledge, no other example is spiral shaped but the reported information from some cerros de trincheras is sketchy at best.

Petroglyphs

Any petroglyphs identified during the 1991 survey were plotted on the site map but no systematic attempt was made to locate rock art or record information on their design characteristics. Harry Crosby (personal communication 1999) has photographed rock art at the site. Design elements include spirals and quadrupeds (Schaafsma 1980:101). Rock art of the Trincheras Tradition is considered a variant of Hohokam styles (Schaafsma 1980; Lindauer and Zaslow 1994; Hayden 1972).

Historic Features

Members of the Pueblo of Trincheras have constructed a trail on the site that leads to a shrine for the Virgin of Guadalupe. The shrine consists of a painting on a cliff face below La Explanada.

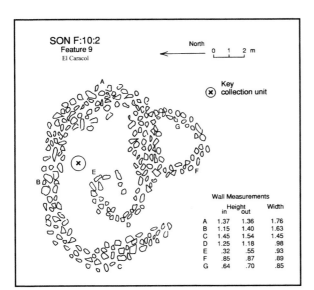

Figure 4.7 Wall Measurements table:

	Height in	Height out	Width
A	1.37	1.36	1.76
B	1.15	1.40	1.63
C	1.45	1.54	1.45
D	1.25	1.18	.98
E	.32	.55	.93
F	.85	.87	.89
G	.64	.70	.85

Figure 4.7   Plan of El Caracol. Drafted by Anne Hull. Courtesy of Randall H. McGuire.

ARTIFACTS

The full analysis of the 24,121 artifacts collected from the surface of Cerro de Trincheras is presented in Appendix A (see also McGuire et al. 1993:40-65). This section contains some summary information on artifact groups and classes relevant for the spatial analysis contained in the following chapter and highlights some interesting general trends in the data.

Ceramics

The primary trends in the ceramic sample are the preponderance of unknown plainware and the low frequency of decorated pottery (Table 4.3). Unknown plainware comprises 55.56% of the total ceramic sample by count and 28.44% by weight, while all plainware constitutes a significant 99.79% of the sample by count. The difference of approximately 27% between count and weight percentages of unknown plainware is indicative of the small average size of the sherds. Small sherd size made both typological and functional identification difficult and the sample of sherds with functional assignments is too small to draw any meaningful conclusions.

Even given the small size of ceramic sherds, very little of the unidentified plainware probably represents the bodies of decorated vessels. Most identified plainware is undeniably of the Trincheras ceramic series and there is little evidence that the unknown plainware is not associated with this series. Trincheras decorated types were executed primarily on Trincheras Plain, variants 1, 1a (McGuire and Villalpando 1993), which comprise a very small percentage of the total identified sample. It is reasonable to assume that decoration was executed on unidentifed plainware, as well. The low percentage of Trincheras decorated types

also confirms this observation (McGuire et al. 1993:43-44).

The ceramic sample suggests interesting circumstances relating to external contact. In general, the low frequency of non-local ceramics indicates that the residents of Cerro de Trincheras were not highly involved in exchange, at least not in goods involving ceramic containers. The small sample of non-local decorated sherds suggests some contact with the Casas Grandes area but there is little evidence for interaction with the Hohokam region. This pattern is repeated in the much larger excavated sample from the site (Gallaga 1997; McGuire et al. 1999; Gallaga and Vargas 2000). Trincheras Plain, variant 3 (designated Thin Plain in the Altar Valley [McGuire and Villalpando 1993:31]) may be connected to interaction within the Trincheras region. This variant is found in relatively low frequencies in the Altar Valley and its connections with other Trincheras ceramics here are uncertain. It is possible that this variant, which occurs in relatively high frequencies at Cerro de Trincheras, was produced at the site and traded into the Altar Valley (Randall H. McGuire, personal communication 1995).

Table 4.3 - Ceramic Types by Count and Weight from All Units

Type	Count	%	Weight (g)	%
Plainware				
Unknown	11763	55.56	11749	28.44
Trincheras Plain 3	8837	41.74	25758	62.36
Late Plain	453	2.14	3194	7.73
Trincheras Plain 1	26	0.12	230	0.56
Trincheras Plain 1a	26	0.12	97	0.24
Trincheras Plain Unidentified	12	0.06	24	0.06
Late Red	12	0.06	70	0.17
Tiburón Plain	1	0.01	2	0.01
Decorated				
Trincheras Purple/Red	12	0.06	55	0.14
Trincheras Purple/Brown	2	0.01	3	0.01
Nogales Polychrome	3	0.01	25	0.06
Babicora Polychrome	3	0.01	13	0.03
Chihuahuan Polychrome	8	0.04	26	0.06
Ramos Polychrome	4	0.02	18	0.04
Santa Cruz Polychrome	9	0.04	40	0.10
Painted Unidentified	1	0.01	3	0.01
Total	21172		41305	

Chipped Stone

The chipped stone assemblage represents an expedient and not very diverse technology. Unmodified waste flakes comprise 84.34% of the total sample (Table 4.4). There was nothing remarkable about the reduction sequence represented with the exception of the relatively low numbers of thinning flakes. This is probably a result of recovery bias associated with surface collection rather than prehistoric production. Site residents appear to have relied heavily on flakes for tasks and activities. The sample contained only 5 formal tools, including a partial San Pedro point, a case of reuse (McGuire et al. 1993:57). The extremely small sample size may be partially due to surface collection by visitors, particularly the relative absence of points. Lithic production and utilization at the site was certainly expedient but we would still expect to find a somewhat higher percentage of formal tools even in this situation. Other tools recovered from the surface survey included unifaces, bifaces, and gravers.

Lithic materials are consistent with expedient production. Most are locally available, igneous, and coarse grained. Basalt is the predominant material type and accounts for 58% of the sample. Rhyolite and quartzite were also used. Fine grained materials are present in very small quantities. Chert flakes comprise only 0.07% of the sample. We did not recover any obsidian artifacts from the site surface.

Table 4.4 - Gross Class Assignments for Chipped Stone

Class	Quantity	%
Waste Flakes	1869	84.34
Utilized\Retouched Flakes	287	12.95
Other	60	2.71
Total	2216	100.00

Note: the other category includes all lithic artifacts accept waste and utilized/retouched flakes, including other tools, such as points, and cores.

Ground Stone

The ground stone sample from Cerro de Trincheras generally exhibits the full range of activities associated with this class of artifacts in the Southwest, from mundane food processing to equally mundane pottery polishing. Most of the sample is comprised of metates and manos and these artifacts provide the most insight into prehistoric activities.

Morphological variation in metates stems from both food processing and jewelry manufacture. The three major metate types at Cerro de Trincheras (Table 4.5) were separated into basic functional categories. Basin metates have been associated with seed grinding (Johnson 1960:155-165) and the concave category resembles trough metates used for agricultural products in the Hohokam area, although they are not as well shaped and have sloping sides. We associate flat metates with jewelry production (McGuire et al. 1993:53). The grinding surfaces of flat metates are poorly defined and they lack a complementary mano type, which would seem to preclude their use for food processing. The shallow, oval grinding patterns on their surfaces are consistent with jewelry production (McGuire et al. 1993:53).

Table 4.5 - Ground Stone Artifacts

Type	Quantity	%
Mano-Loaf	16	11.85
Mano-2 sided	11	8.15
Mano-3 sided	1	0.74
Mano-Square	1	0.74
Mano-Irregular	3	2.22
Mano-Unidentified	2	1.48
Metate-Flat	45	33.33
Metate-Concave	20	14.81
Metate-Basin	5	3.70
Metate-Fixed	2	1.48
Metate-Unidentified	9	6.67
Lapstone	9	6.67
Tabular Knife	2	1.48
Pestle	3	2.22
Stone Vessel	1	0.74
Polishing Stone	1	0.74
Axe-3/4 grooved	1	0.74
Unidentified	3	2.22
Total	135	100.00

Flat metates comprised one third of the total ground stone sample and were more numerous than basin and concave metates combined (Table 4.5). The high frequency of flat metates does present some interpretative problems because it is difficult to imagine jewelry production taking precedence over basic subsistence needs. Shell exchange does not seem to have been an important factor at the site. Therefore, we would not expect an inordinately high investment in production related artifacts. It is possible that we are in error and flat metates were used for activities other than jewelry production. Alternatively, basin and concave metates may have seen more post-occupation reuse and removal. Excavation data should help us resolve these questions.

The surface survey did locate other ground stone artifacts and features associated with jewelry manufacture. We recovered 9 lapstones from the site. Several dozen bedrock metates were also noted in the northwestern portion of the main hill. The bedrock metates are small, shallow depressions, measuring 2-5 cm deep. They appear to have been used for light grinding activities, which may include jewelry production (McGuire et al. 1993:51).

One other interesting characteristic of the ground stone sample is the presence of two tabular knives, which may have been used to process agave and yucca. It has been suggested that these two plants were grown on terraces (Downum et al. 1994:283). The preliminary results from the flotation analysis of the excavation data confirm the presence of agave at the site, although its cultivation on terraces has not been firmly established.

Shell

The distribution of general categories of shell artifacts provides some insight into production. Finished pieces comprise 27.76% of the sample, debitage makes up 66.05%, and raw material represents 5.18% of the shell sample (Table 4.6). The small amount of raw material suggests that pieces were roughed out at the source and only finishing work was done at the site (McGuire et al. 1993:59). Once raw material arrived at the site, it appears to have been worked to exhaustion (McGuire et al. 1993:64). Nearly a third of the debitage could not be associated with a specific product due to the small size of the fragments, due to the heavy use of grinding in the production process. Finished pieces are primarily bracelets (Table 4.7). The size of the sample and its general composition has led our analyst to conclude that shell was produced for local consumption (McGuire et al. 1993:59-65).

SUMMARY

The diversity of the architectural remains and the general nature of the artifact assemblage documented by the 1991 survey clearly indicate that Cerro de Trincheras was not a specialized, limited use site. All major categories of artifacts associated with town sites in the Northwest/Southwest (e.g., Haury 1976) are present at the site in sufficient quantities to indicate permanent habitation. General characteristics of site artifact data provide more specific information on daily life at Cerro de Trincheras and also indicate that populations at

Table 4.6 - Gross Shell Categories

Gross Category	Quantity	%
Finished Pieces	166	27.76
Debitage	395	66.05
Raw Material	31	5.18
Unknown	4	0.67
Natural	2	0.33
Total	598	100.00

Table 4.7 - Finished Shell Artifacts

Type	Quantity	%
Bracelet	90	54.22
Pendent	34	20.48
Ring	30	18.07
Bead	11	6.63
Figurine	1	0.60
Total	166	100.00

the site were not heavily involved in long distance exchange of shell, lithics, or other commodities transported in ceramic containers. The nature of daily life and activities and their organization is more thoroughly explored through the analysis of broad scale patterning at Cerro de Trincheras in the following chapter.

Chapter Five
Site Organization and Structure

The analysis of the surface artifact and architectural data focused on reconstructing broad scale activity patterns and organization at Cerro de Trincheras. The artifact distribution and architectural analysis generally indicate that there were specific zones primarily devoted to domestic, ritual, and agricultural utilization. They also provide some clues regarding the social dimensions of production and ritual organization. Discrete clusters of residential terraces seem to be indicative of larger social groupings, probably based on kinship. It is not unreasonable to assume that much of daily life revolved around kin relations, but how these intermeshed with ritual and other community relations is still unclear. Ritual architecture on the crest suggests some control of access that must have translated into some differences in social power.

ARTIFACT ANALYSIS

The artifact analysis concentrated on surface distributions of artifact types. Patterns in artifact distribution at the site are probably the result of refuse deposition on terraces and its reuse as construction fill. Refuse deposition on terraces occurred either in or near activity areas or at the back of terraces. In both cases refuse is generally associated with its area of use. Refuse was also used in construction fill, which presented the most complex interpretative problem. However, using several assumptions regarding the composition and dimensions of probable construction fill, it was possible to separate patterning related to use of an area from that related to construction to some extent.

Methodology

Reconstructing the broad scale activity structure of Cerro de Trincheras required linking artifact analysis files to the spatial coordinates of the artifact collection and count units to produce distribution information. Geo-Map used an interpolative process on the aerial images used for field mapping. This technique did not produce a data layer with specific coordinates for artifact units, which required the digitizing of artifact units. The coordinate file produced through digitization in AutoCAD was translated into a data base format that would link to the artifact files. The data files with linked artifact units and frequencies were then transferred to the Surfer© mapping program.

Surfer© produces isometric plots relating x, y, and z coordinates, in this case spatial coordinates and unit artifact frequency. The isometric plots were created using the inverse distance method for calculating appropriate connections between spatially separate data points. The inverse distance method weights data points to decrease the effect of outliers on data contours. For this analysis the default weight value of 2 was used (Golden Software 1990:26-27).

The final step in this process was linking the isometric plots to the site map to produce overlays. The figures produced for this report use a base site map produced by Geo-Map that has been reduced in scale and edited to show only major site topography and features.

Artifact Sampling and Data Sets

The site sampling strategy the Cerro de Trincheras Mapping Project employed (see Chapter Four) resulted in two data sets with different levels of information. Artifact class frequencies from all survey units are found in table 5.1. Artifacts within each class were counted and recorded in the field. A systematic sample of these survey units was selected for further analysis (see Chapter Four). Frequency by artifact class from these units is shown in (Table 5.2). Analysis included assessments of artifact and material type and recording of dimensional information. Thus, the collected artifact sample includes data on types within each artifact class, for example, the number of waste flakes present in the lithic sample, materials used, and size. The only artifact class that was not collected for further analysis was bone due to its possible origin in cremation burials. Survey crews divided bone into burnt and unburnt categories in the field and noted the frequency of each on the recording form.

A brief comparison of tables 5.1 and 5.2 reveals that the unit sample of shell and ground stone is less than the collected sample. This discrepancy is due to our use of a total recording strategy for these two artifact classes (see Chapter Four). Distribution plots of shell and ground stone, to be discussed shortly, are based on the frequency data shown in table 5.2, since they better convey artifact patterning and primarily depart from the plots of the unit sample in magnitude, not form. Analysis of the collected sample of ground stone and shell was based on terrace provenience due to the occurrence of some of these artifacts outside collection or count units. Distribution plots of other classes of artifacts, such as ceramics and lithics, and categories within these, are based on the controlled data from survey units and can be provenienced by both terrace and unit, for example, T-607, unit 3.

Artifact Distributions

Total Artifacts
The isometric plot of total artifacts shows seven distinct artifact clusters (Figure 5.1), most of which are located on the north face of the main hill (clusters 1-4). Two of the seven clusters are located on the western side of the site, one on the main hill below El Pico de Zopilotes (cluster 6) and the other encompassing part of the hill and the area near Cerrito del Oeste (cluster 5). The seventh cluster is a small concentration of artifacts surrounding Cerrito del Sur and corresponds to the edge of a known pit house village, most of which lies beyond the currently mapped site boundary.

The clusters vary somewhat in composition (Table 5.3). All of the clusters primarily consist of ceramics. However, clusters 4 and 5 have much higher relative percentages of lithic artifacts. The ratio of ceramics to lithics in the total artifact sample is 8 to 1, but in clusters 4 and 5 the ratio of ceramics to lithics is 3 to 1. The remaining clusters have ceramic to lithic ratios close to that of the total sample.

Ceramics
The ceramic distribution largely mirrors the same spatial pattern of total artifacts, therefore, it is not reproduced here. The correspondence between these two distributions is not surprising, given the high frequency of ceramics in the total sample (see Table 5.1).

The distribution of ceramic types is equally uninformative because the collected ceramic sample primarily consists of unknown plainwares. Nearly all identified plainware belongs to the Trincheras ceramic series, in particular Trincheras Plain, variant 3 (see Table 4.3). The Trincheras series is not well known, or dated, making patterns difficult to assess. The collected ceramic sample does contain some intrusive ceramics that might yield insights into social organization and

Table 5.1 - Frequency of Artifact Classes
from All Units

Artifact Class	Quantity	%
Ceramics	44062	88.28
Lithics	5543	11.11
Shell	175	0.35
Ground Stone	38	0.08
Burnt Bone	75	0.15
Bone	21	0.04
Total	49914	100.00

Table 5.2 - Frequency of Artifact Classes
in the Collected Sample

Artifact Class	Quantity	%
Ceramics	21172	87.77
Lithics	2216	9.19
Shell	598	2.48
Ground Stone	135	0.56
Total	24121	100.00

Table 5.3 - Composition of Total Artifact Clusters

Cluster No.	Ceramics	Lithics	Other	Total
1	90.49	8.71	0.80	10415
2	92.58	7.33	0.09	2196
3	94.15	5.58	0.27	1488
4	78.17	21.26	0.57	701
5	74.65	24.34	1.00	1483
6	95.45	4.55	0	988
7	85.92	13.81	0.27	1108
Total				49845

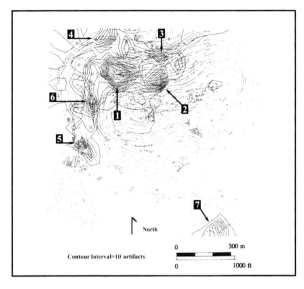

Figure 5.1   Distribution of total artifacts.

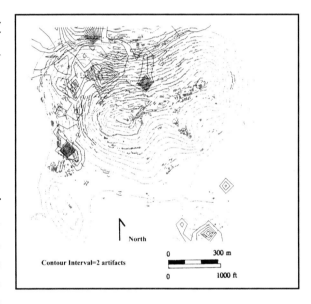

Figure 5.2   Distribution of lithics.

exchange but the sample is too small to draw any definite conclusions. The 24 intrusive sherds primarily occur in the northwestern portion of the main cerro, but this area has higher artifact frequencies in general. A few exotic sherds were also recovered from Terrace 1 at the base of Cerrito del Sur.

Lithics

The general lithic distribution has three major clusters on the main hill and a small one in the area of the pit house village (Figure 5.2). Two of the lithic clusters occur near clusters 4 and 5 in the total artifact sample, which have comparatively higher lithic frequencies (Table 5.3). Cluster 5 of the to-

tal artifact sample shows a more exact correspondence with the lithic distribution than does cluster 4, where the lithic cluster is offset slightly to the east. The third lithic cluster on the main hill is located within cluster 2 in the total artifact sample. This was one of four clusters in the total artifact distribution that had ceramic frequencies above 90% (Table 5.3) and we would not expect large numbers of lithics here. The cluster probably reflects a concentration of lithic activity within a relatively low frequency area. Lower frequency contours in the lithic distribution also extend across much of the northwestern portion of the site.

The composition of the lithic clusters is illustrated by distributions of general lithic categories from the collected sample. Waste flakes tend to concentrate in areas of high lithic frequency, although this is less obvious in the case of the lithic concentration in cluster 2 of the total artifact distribution (Figure 5.3). Utilized and retouched flakes have a much more diffuse distribution with less definite clustering (Figure 5.4), although some do occur near areas of high lithic frequency. The actual number of utilized and retouched flakes in any area is relatively small in comparison to waste flakes.

Tools, such as unifaces and gravers, comprise too small a sample for an isometric plot. These artifacts tend to concentrate on the north face of the main hill but no portion of this area has a significantly higher frequency. A few other areas, such as Cerrito del Sur and the crest of the main hill, also have a few examples of tools. The small sample size precludes any conclusions regarding the distribution of tools.

Ground Stone
The distribution of ground stone from survey units and the collected sample have relatively similar spatial plots, therefore only the collected sample is illustrated here (Figure 5.5). The isometric plot shows two primary clusters, which represent peaks in a more diffuse distribution that flows from the north face onto the western side of the hill. One falls within cluster 1 in the total artifact distribution and the other encompasses cluster 6 in this distribution and extends farther south and east. They are linked by lower level contours that wrap around La Explanada between the northern and western faces of the hill.

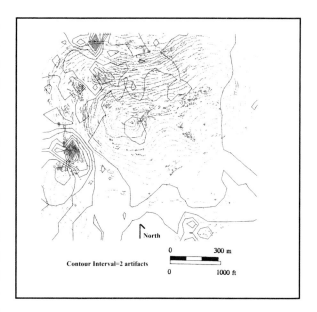

Figure 5.3   Distribution of waste flakes.

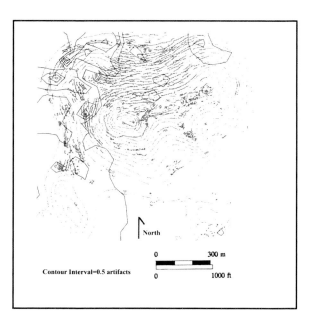

Figure 5.4   Distribution of utilized flakes.

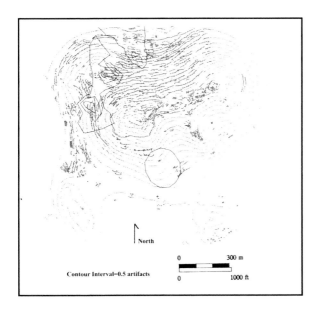

Figure 5.5   Distribution of ground stone.

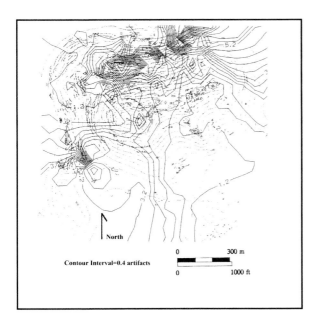

Figure 5.6   Distribution of shell.

The concentration of ground stone near La Explanada with its numerous bedrock metates is suggestive of some type of processing area. Both jewelry manufacturing and food processing ground stone artifacts occur within the two clusters and are relatively evenly represented. No category of ground stone artifacts is present in either cluster in frequencies higher than its relative proportion in the total artifact sample. It is possible that our assessment of flat metates as jewelry manufacturing items is inaccurate. However, the shallow wear patterns and lack of a corresponding mano certainly favor the jewelry manufacturing interpretation. Given this, the association of both artifact types suggests that food and jewelry production were performed within the same general context.

Two other small clusters within the isometric plot of ground stone occur on the main cerro. One is located below and to the east of La Explanada at the lower elevations of the north face of the main cerro. The other is on the south side of the hill. Only four scattered artifacts are represented.

Shell

The collected shell sample and the survey unit sample had approximately the same distribution. Only the collected sample is used here because it displays more detail (Figure 5.6). The major peaks in the distribution encompass a large portion of the middle to lower reaches of the north face and also occur on the western side of the hill near cluster 5 of the total artifact distribution. Shell artifact clusters on the north face of the main cerro overlap clusters 1 and 3 of the total artifact distribution. The shell cluster in the area of cluster 1 of the total artifact distribution extends below its boundary but the one near cluster 3 essentially corresponds to it. The shell cluster near cluster 5 in the total artifact distribution is located slightly southeast of it. The remaining peaks in the shell distribution occur on the far, lower portion of eastern side of the north face. All of the major peaks are connected by lower level contours that extend across much of the site, indicating a relatively unrestricted distribution.

The general categories of shell artifacts include manufacturing debitage, manufactured pieces, and raw material. Generally, all categories coincide with the major clusters in the shell distribution (Figures 5.7-5.9). Debitage (Figure 5.7) has a more diffuse distribution on the north face that extends farther up into terraces below the crest than does the general shell distribution. Manufactured pieces (Figure 5.8) fall within shell clusters on the northern face and the western slope. Raw material, which has a very small sample size, is primarily concentrated in the easternmost shell cluster on the north face (Figure 5.9).

The distributions of general shell categories indicate that only one of the clusters in the general shell distribution contains notable quantities of each category. This is the cluster located on the eastern portion of the north face. But the effect of sample sizes on the distributions must be considered in assessing the composition of the shell clusters. Distinct clusters may not be present in areas of very low concentration. The raw material sample is quite small, containing only 31 artifacts. Raw material is certainly present in small quanti-

ties in the western portion of the north face and this might be magnified with a larger sample. The dense cluster of manufactured pieces on the western side of the site near Cerrito del Oeste consists of eight items out of a total of 22 shell artifacts found in this area. Debitage actually occurs more frequently in this area comprising 13 of the 22 total artifacts, but is only evidenced as a small peak due to its larger sample size and generally more

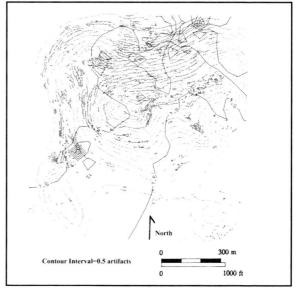

Figure 5.8   Distribution of manufactured shell items.

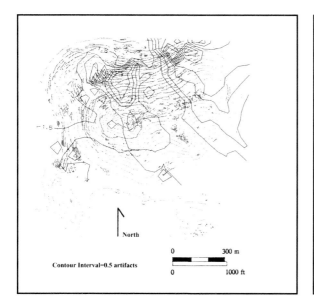

Figure 5.7   Distribution of shell debitage.

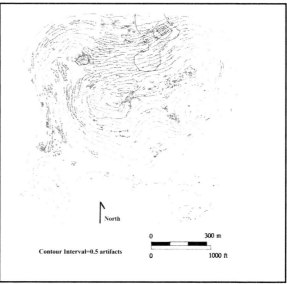

Figure 5.9   Distribution of shell raw material.

dispersed distribution. The remaining single shell artifact from this cluster is a piece of raw material.

Bone

Bone is the last major category of artifacts noted on the site. Field crews did not collect bone for analysis and it was not identified to species or taxa. The burnt bone sample, which could derive from cremation burials or domestic contexts, shows two

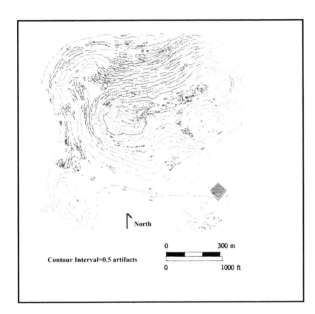

Figure 5.10   *Distribution of burnt bone.*

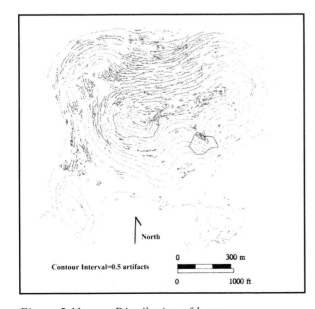

Figure 5.11   *Distribution of bone.*

major clusters (Figure 5.10). One occurs on the north side of the main hill within cluster 1 of the total artifact distribution. The second, located near Cerrito del Sur, corresponds to a known cremation cemetery. Most of the bone from here and the north face is calcined, typical of human cremations (McGuire 1994). Looter's holes have exposed the remains of several burials near Cerrito del Sur. Based on sherds exposed by the looters our best estimation is that the cremation cemetery is contemporaneous with the main hill occupation. However, dating at the site is still very imprecise.

Although the bone sample is extremely small, n=21, an isometric plot indicates one cluster (Figure 5.11). The cluster corresponds to scattered terraces on the south side of the main hill and the complex of terraces on El Borde de Sur. No terrace contains more than a handful of bone fragments and it is difficult to draw conclusions from this small sample.

Artifact Patterning and Site Organization

Artifact distributions indicate several interesting patterns that may be linked to the organization of production and residential life at Cerro de Trincheras. However, they cannot be taken at face value. Natural and cultural formation processes have affected surface artifact distributions, therefore they must be considered before interpreting the patterns discussed in the previous sections.

Formation Processes

The most significant natural formation processes that would have affected surface artifact distributions are erosion and faunalturbation. The impact of water and wind erosion on artifact patterning is always a consideration in hillside contexts. In its unmodified state the hill that the site occupies would be a fairly active erosional area. The thin, light, desert soils on steep slopes would offer little resistance to erosional agents. We have not made systematic observations of the rate of erosion at Cerro de Trincheras but the erosional potential of the unmodified hill is considerably lessened by cultural terracing. Terrace walls of several meters in height found in the areas of highest average slope form a barrier that slows and prevents the downslope movement of artifacts and soil. The depth of the terrace fill behind these high walls would also act to increase water absorption, slowing run-off. Some downslope movement of artifacts must have occurred but major displacements of large numbers of artifacts is not likely. Erosion probably displaced artifacts on a terrace and between adjacent terraces. Any resultant downslope movement would affect interpretations of small, specific areas of the site but not broad scale patterning.

Faunalturbation is a known source of artifact movement within sites. Burrowing animals can move small artifacts from deeper contexts to the surface through tunneling activities (Schiffer 1987:207-210), but they do not generally move artifacts between terraces. The surface of Cerro de Trincheras exhibits animal burrows but their contribution to the general artifact patterning is probably minimal. Survey crews avoided areas near animal burrows. It is unlikely that more than a minute fraction of the nearly 50,000 artifacts from the site were distributed by faunalturbation.

Cultural formation processes present more complex interpretative challenges for associating artifacts with their context of use. Artifact patterning at the site is probably the result of at least three cultural formation processes: deposition of refuse on terraces near the context of use, deposition of refuse in trash dumps at the back of the terrace, and the use of trash for construction fill. Excavations at the site in 1995 and 1996 revealed that some terrace platforms were constructed of rocks, soil, and trash (McGuire 1997). Stratigraphic profiles of the trash-filled terraces indicate that hard packed occupation surfaces were present above the construction fill. Before being used as construction fill, refuse is usually allowed to decompose to prevent slumping (Schiffer 1987). It is likely, then,

that the refuse component of construction fill at Cerro de Trincheras originated as secondary refuse.

Excavation data indicate that surface artifact distributions and patterning reflect a complex depositional history. We have currently only excavated approximately 1.5% of the site (McGuire et al. 1999) and do not have sufficient information to sort out a construction sequence and relate this to depositional events. Several excavated terraces with trash fill occurred in areas of high surface artifact density. Artifact patterning in these areas could stem from a mix of all relevant deposition processes, including construction fill. Construction fill presents the most significant problem for the interpretation of artifact patterning as it could have originated from many scattered locations. General refuse was deposited on a terrace and in terrace dumps near their context of use and thus can be linked to activities in an area. To reconstruct broad scale activity patterning a number of measures and assumptions were used to tease out the contributions of various types of refuse.

Interpreting Artifact Patterning
The small sample of excavated terraces from the site provides us with only limited information on areas where trash was used as part of the construction fill. Most distributions of specific artifact classes and categories tend to occur within or near high density clusters in the total artifact distribution, possibly representing mixed contexts in which construction fill is potentially present. Nevertheless, several principles can be used to separate patterning related to activities performed in an area from that stemming from construction fill. The density and diversity of total artifact clusters can provide some information on the nature of depositional processes involved. Comparisons of specific artifact distributions with the total artifact distribution, and the presence of very small or large artifacts can also furnish some inferences regarding occupation and activities. For example, dis-

crete clusters within a cluster in the total artifact distribution and very small artifacts unlikely to be discarded as trash, probably represent activities that occurred in an area. On excavated trash filled terraces, the fill level began approximately 10-20 cm below the surface. In general, therefore, it is also safe to assume that artifacts are more likely to have originated in deposits closer to the surface, which are probably derived from occupation levels above the construction fill.

The excavated terraces within cluster 1 of the total artifact sample contain trash fill but the existence of other potential areas of trash fill must be inferred. Density comparisons provide one possible measure of mixed deposits (Schiffer 1987:325-326), although they cannot be used uncritically because density can be affected by many processes, including reuse. Comparisons of surface artifact densities, however, provide a rough indication of potential areas of construction fill, intensive occupation, or both.

Within the total artifact distribution artifact densities for clusters range from approximately 13 to 105 artifacts/m² (Table 5.4). The average artifact density for the site is 19.8 artifacts/m². The artifact density of cluster 1, where trash fill was used for at least some terrace construction, is nearly five times the site average. Clusters 2 and 3, also on the north face of the main hill and cluster 5, located on the western slope outside the densely terraced north face, have similarly high densities and may also contain trash fill. However, increased artifact densities in these areas may also

stem from extremely intensive or long-term occupation. Given our current understanding of the site, a more conservative approach that assumes clusters 1, 2, 3, and 5 represent an uncertain mix of primary and secondary refuse from terrace trash dumps and construction fill is warranted.

The lower densities in clusters 4 and 6 may indicate of a lack of trash used as construction fill in these areas. Cluster 4 is located at the lower elevations of the site, an area of relatively flat topography. Sufficient fill for the low walled terraces in this area could have been easily obtained from surrounding soil and rock. Cluster 6 encompasses relatively substantial terraces higher on the hill and low artifact densities here are suggestive of occupational refuse since we would expect higher artifact densities similar to those in cluster 1 if trash was used in construction fill. Cluster 7 in the area of the pit house occupation is an extremely low density area that only stands out due to the general lack of intensive utilization of the surrounding area.

Some inferences may still be drawn from mixed contexts, such as cluster 1 of the total artifact sample, by examining composition and patterning. Secondary refuse contexts vary according to occupational length and source of the refuse. The composition of secondary refuse from sites occupied over long spans of time or at which a wide range of activities occurred, tends to be more diverse than that of short term, limited activity contexts (Schiffer 1987:282). The span of occupation at Cerro de Trincheras is approximately 150 years (McGuire et al. 1999). In addition, the artifact sample is consistent with a generalized habitation context (see Chapter Four). Given this, secondary refuse in general should be relatively diverse. Refuse from specific activities, such as that from a lithic manufacturing area, would not be as diverse as that deriving from general habitation (Schiffer 1987:282) and may form discrete clusters. These clusters are more likely to stem from activities in their area of deposition than to have

Table 5.4 - Densities in Peak Artifact Areas

Cluster No. within Total Artifact Distribution	Artifacts/m²
1	89.68
2	73.15
3	85.62
4	52.20
5	104.29
6	36.78
7	12.64

originated in construction fill. Trash used for construction fill was probably allowed to cure in secondary refuse contexts before use (Schiffer 1987:70) and would be mixed with dirt, rocks, and secondary refuse from other contexts during construction. The probability that discrete artifact clusters within secondary refuse retained their integrity during this process is relatively low. In addition, for distinct surface clusters to have originated in construction fill, they must have been selectively displaced to the surface as a relatively intact unit after deposition. No known natural agents or cultural processes would entail such activity. Thus, artifact distributions with distinct concentrations within peak areas in the total artifact distribution or large concentrations can be linked to activities in the area. Small clusters probably stem from higher disposal rates in terrace dumps related to activities in that area. Large artifact clusters encompassing dozens of terraces and tens of meters of elevation are also unlikely to have originated in construction fill, because the source of this fill would have to be exceedingly large and uniform. Although such deposits may have existed, this patterning is more parsimoniously explained as refuse associated with these areas.

The distribution of certain sizes of artifacts presents another interpretive avenue. Small artifacts are more likely to remain in their context of use than to be redeposited as either secondary refuse or construction fill (Schiffer 1987:62). Waste flakes form the largest group of artifacts for which size data exist. The presence of very small waste flakes, those less than 1 cm^2, may be indicative of refuse deposited in or near the context of use (Figure 5.12). Ground stone artifacts, particularly metates, may represent activity areas rather than construction fill. Although metates and manos were used in the construction fill, it is unlikely that these large, heavy artifacts were displaced to the surface or selectively redeposited in quantity at any distance from their contexts of use.

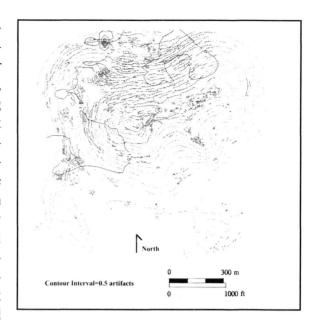

Figure 5.12   Distribution of small waste flakes.

Activity Zones and Occupation

The best evidence of domestic utilization comes from artifact density, diversity, and more specifically, food processing artifacts, such as ground stone. Domestic contexts should have high artifact diversity due to their generalized nature (Schiffer 1987:282) and high artifact densities stemming from secondary refuse disposal at the back of occupied terraces. The clusters (1,2,3 and 5) within the total artifact distribution on the northwest face of main hill probably mark areas of domestic occupation. All have higher than average artifact densities that may stem from a mix of occupational refuse and construction fill. Most major artifact classes occur within their confines. Additional evidence that some portion of this area was used for domestic purposes is provided by the ground stone distribution. Food processing activities are typically carried out within households in the Northwest/Southwest and there is no reason to believe that concentrations of metates and manos would be associated with limited use areas. Ground stone tends to concentrate around

La Explanada on the northwest face of the main hill, crossing the upper portion of cluster 1 in the total artifact distribution and encompassing cluster 6. A smaller cluster in the distribution occurs in the lower reaches of the northwest face of the main hill, outside the most intensive total artifact concentrations.

The known pit house village located south of Cerrito del Sur is indicated by peaks in the total artifact, ceramic, and lithic distributions. Seven to ten pit houses were excavated during the 1995 season (McGuire 1997). Radiocarbon dates suggest that the pit house village was contemporaneous with the main hill occupation, approximately A.D. 1300-1450 (McGuire et al. 1999), but we have so few dates for either context that we cannot be confident of this assessment. The pit house component was never a major residential area. Surface evidence of pit house constructions and the artifact scatter area indicate that it consists of roughly 35 pit houses, not all of which would have been occupied simultaneously (McGuire et al. 1993).

The pit house village is located to the south of a cremation cemetery exposed by looting. This cemetery may be associated with the cerro, pit house village population, or both. One concentration of burnt bone that overlaps the eastern half of cluster 1 of the total artifact distribution may also represent a cremation area. Burnt bone was not collected for analysis but field observations suggest that it was cremated human bone, since it was burned white and highly fragmented. Animal bone is usually not subjected to the high temperatures that produce such characteristics (McGuire 1994). It is unlikely that small, scattered fragments of human cremations that may have escaped burial and ended up in construction fill would maintain their integrity and be manifested as a discrete surface cluster. Burnt bone here probably represents one or more cremation burials or a small cemetery. Two exotic sherds recovered within the burnt bone

concentration lend additional support to this interpretation. The probable cemetery, or cremation area, could stem from groups resident at the site, and perhaps resident within that area. Alternatively, it could be a post-occupational intrusion, although this is unlikely. Other intrusive burials at the site are inhumations.

High artifact density areas may have obscured evidence of occupation in other areas. The eastern side of the north face and southern face of the main cerro have artifact densities of 3.87 and $5.04/m^2$, respectively. These densities are well below the site average; however, both areas have indications of some occupation. On the eastern side of the north face, the distribution of small flakes shows a diffuse scatter in this area, highlighting the occurrence of some refuse related to lithic production here, if not more generalized habitation. Both areas are also as densely terraced as some areas with high artifact densities, such as clusters 5 and 6 in the total artifact distribution.

Possible explanations for low artifact densities center on site occupation history and construction sequence. The presence of trash fill in high density areas would certainly raise the average artifact density and may have skewed general impressions of artifact densities across the site. Alternatively, an earlier occupation may have occurred in low density areas and accumulated trash was used in subsequent constructions or low density areas may have been less intensively occupied and used. Finally, differences in activities may explain the low densities in these areas despite their lack of architectural distinctiveness from more generalized domestic contexts. The evidence for lithic manufacturing on the eastern side of the north face may indicate more specialized use of the area; however, only small waste flakes concentrate here and lithic manufacturing debris does not generally occur in large quantities.

Other areas of low artifact density are definitely related to differences in the activities performed in them. Major portions of the surveyed sections surrounding the base of the hill have very low artifact densities, less than 10 artifacts/square meter. Few features occur in this area, although narrow terraces, which were probably used for agriculture, are found here. The relative lack of features, low artifact densities, and the occurrence of narrow terraces indicate that this was not a primary residential area. The crest of the hill has an average artifact density of 6.84 artifacts/m^2 and yet the area surveyed and collected on the crest is actually larger than that of all seven clusters within the total artifact distribution. In this case, the area appears to have been used for ritual activities and, unsurprisingly, was kept relatively clean. Both the agricultural use of terraces and ritual features are more fully explored in the architectural section.

Shell Manufacture and Organization

The general distribution of shell artifacts indicates that these items were quite widely available. Moreover, the distribution of debitage indicates that production was not restricted. Both shell artifacts and debitage tend to concentrate on the western side of the north face and near cluster 5 of the total artifact distribution but lower level contours also extend over much of the densely terraced northern face. The distribution of raw material is more restricted, with one major cluster at the lower elevations of the extreme eastern edge of the north face and a small cluster that falls within cluster 1 of the total artifact sample. The raw material sample is relatively small, however, and may not be an adequate indicator of restricted access. Some of the initial stages of shell manufacture may have been performed off-site, because material brought to the site seems to have been heavily worked (Appendix A; see also McGuire et al. 1993:64). The broad distribution of shell artifacts indicates that production and access were not highly controlled; however, shell artifacts are found in higher frequencies in specific areas. High density areas of shell within this broad distribution may signal some de-

gree of differential involvement in production or access to finished products by specific groups or individuals at Cerro de Trincheras. The shell debitage distribution shows three major peak areas: the western portion of the northern face, at its extreme eastern edge, and on the lower slopes near cluster 5. Debitage in the western portion encompasses cluster 1 and portions of cluster 2 of the total artifact distribution and extends beyond major artifact concentrations into the terraces below El Pico de Zopilotes. The probability of such a large, coherent debitage cluster originating in construction fill is relatively low and it is possible that shell was manufactured over a large portion of the north face. Manufactured pieces and raw material also occur in this area. The shell concentration near cluster 5 of the total artifact distribution contains eight manufactured items and 22 pieces of debitage. The lack of exact correspondence between shell clusters and the total artifact cluster here signals a discrete artifact concentration that may by due to production. The best evidence for production in the area is the occurrence of one of the flat metates associated with jewelry production. The small amount of shell recovered from this area clearly indicates only minor involvement in production. The concentration of debitage, raw material, and finished pieces at the extreme eastern edge of the north face is outside other artifact concentrations. This concentration of shell occurs just east of La Cancha, one of the large ritual features at the site and it is tempting to associate production and use of shell in this area with activities in La Cancha. However, the area has been bulldozed (see Chapter Four), which certainly moved artifacts vertically and horizontally. Therefore, it is impossible to draw any conclusions regarding artifact patterning in this area.

The two areas of high shell density other than that near La Cancha indicate that shell production is associated with domestic contexts. The convergence of ground stone and shell around La Explanada provides further insight into the organization of shell ornament production. Ground stone clusters in this area contain both basin metates, associated with food production and flat metates, which have been interpreted as related to jewelry production. Over half of the lapstone sample also occurs here and numerous bedrock metates, or metate slicks (Schaasfma 1980:96), are found on La Explanada. The shallow, small depressions that form the bedrock metates were probably not produced through food processing activities and it is more likely that they are related to jewelry manufacture. This evidence suggests relatively intensive shell production in this area at the household level or within a group of related households, a not uncommon occurrence in the larger region (Seymour 1988).

Lithic Production
Chipped stone tends to concentrate in three areas of the site: at the lower elevations of the northern and western slopes of the main cerro and at the higher elevations of the northern face within cluster 2 of the total artifact distribution. The concentration of lithics in the first two areas probably stems from lithic production activities in these areas, since they are near and within clusters 4 and 5 of the total artifact distribution that had higher than average ceramic to lithic ratios. If the lithic artifacts in these areas are a result of trash fill, we might expect the ratio of ceramics to lithics to correspond more closely with that of the total sample. Also, terrace construction at these lower elevations is less likely to require trash fill as the low walled constructions here could have been filled primarily with adjacent soil and rock. The distribution of small waste flakes also clusters within these areas, offering further evidence of lithic reduction and production.

A third cluster in the small waste flake distribution occurs in the upper elevations of the northwest face within cluster 1 of the total artifact distribution and may be representative of some lithic manufacturing. The lithic concentration within

cluster 2 of the total artifact distribution is relatively discrete and is also probably a result of lithic production in this area.

The higher frequency of lithic manufacturing debris in some areas of the site may be a result of more intensive production, specific activities, higher disposal rates, or any combination of these factors. The expedient nature of the lithic assemblage and the low quality of the materials used makes the association of any specific activities difficult. Use-wear analysis of the basalt, rhyolite, and quartzite that comprise most of the lithic sample has proven unproductive in the past and was not conducted on the survey sample.

Summary of Artifact Data

Artifact patterning suggests that residential areas on the main hill tend to concentrate in the northwestern area. High density peaks within the total artifact distribution are probably due to a combination of residential activity and trash fill. More definitive evidence of domestic contexts on the main hill is provided by the concentration of ground stone, including food processing artifacts, along La Explanada. A small cluster of ground stone also occurs at lower elevations on the northern face. Some of the high density areas on the northern and western slopes show evidence of lithic manufacture. Sections of the main cerro, particularly its extreme eastern edge, have very low artifact densities, although there are some indications that these areas could also have been used for residential purposes. Low artifact densities in these areas may stem from the differential distribution of trash fill, less intensive occupation, or an as yet undetermined variation in activities. Other areas of low artifact density, such as the crest, probably relate to specialized use.

Spatial patterning of shell artifacts provides some evidence regarding specific productive activities and the organization of production. The correspondence of shell jewelry manufacturing debris with food processing artifacts and the concentration of shell debitage in potential residential areas suggest that production generally occurred at the household level. The concentration of the shell at the eastern edge of the north face may or may not be a special instance where production occurred near a ritual area. The broad distribution of debitage and manufactured pieces across the site is not indicative of control by an elite group or groups. Most shell was probably produced for local on-site consumption, given the general quantity of shell present, and not exchange (see Chapter Four and Appendix A; see also McGuire et al. 1993). This observation is borne out at the local level by a recent analysis that indicates other site populations were producing shell for their own consumption (Vargas 2000).

Shell is associated with elite status in the Northwest-Southwest (McGuire and Howard 1987) and differential involvement in its manufacture or the distribution of finished items may have implications for social organization and structure. However, the exact nature of any social differences and inequities related to shell production is difficult to determine with the surface data. The most that can be inferred from these data is that differential involvement in the production of, and access to, shell artifacts may indicate some slight distinctions in wealth and status but not control.

The evidence from the artifact distributions forms only half of the interpretative equation. Architectural arrangement is also indicative of site patterning and organization and can add depth and certainty to conclusions drawn from artifact data. Architectural analysis indicates that the site was divided into broad activity zones of domestic, agricultural, and ritual activities.

ARCHITECTURE AND ORGANIZATION

The arrangement of distinct classes of architectural features indicates that the north face was the primary residential area and that two ritual areas existed, one on the crest and one at La Cancha. Agricultural activities primarily occurred on the more level ground surrounding the main hill. This broad structure can be further refined by examining patterning within specific feature types. Grouped arrangements of terraces are suggestive of a social unit above the household level. The two ritual areas of the site display varying degrees of control and access to knowledge and rites that relate to the conditions and circumstances of social inequities and power.

Residential Areas and Organization

Terraces are the most numerous architectural class and residential structures were located on them. The 1995 and 1996 excavation data indicate the presence of ephemeral domestic structures on terraces. These structures probably had a jacal superstructure of ocotillo and daub (McGuire et al. 1999). Circular stone structures, the next most numerous architectural class, are predominately associated with terraces and, in these cases, may have served as domestic spaces. Quadrangular stone structures occur in low frequency, and most are isolates. Although at least some of these features were used as rooms, they are certainly not the principal form of residential architecture.

All of the approximately 900 terraces at Cerro de Trincheras did not support dwellings. Certain terraced areas appear to have been used for special activities, such as the crest, and others are not large enough for even a small domestic structure. Using a minimum width of 2 m the estimated number of residential terraces is 719 (McGuire et al. 1993:72). This estimate is, however, too high since the number of terraces it excludes does not allow for the amount of variability in activities that assessments of the architectural and organizational structure of the site seem to indicate. Width would seem to be the crucial variable for construction on a hillside but the unrealistic estimate produced using only width indicates that length probably also played a role in residential usage. Residential structures in the region are frequently associated with outdoor activity areas, such as ramadas. Ramada areas on terraces may have principally involved terrace length due to the limitations placed on expansion in width by the nature of hillside construction. Terraces with structures at Linda Vista Hill in the Tucson Basin had a minimum width of 2 m and a length of approximately 15 m (Downum 1986). Cerro de Trincheras has 422 terraces that fall within a 2 by 15 m dimensional parameter, a figure that seems too low given that it would imply that over half the terraces at the site were non-residential (McGuire et al. 1993:72-73). While this may be the case, it does beg the question of why residents built more non-residential than residential terraces. The true number of residential terraces probably lies somewhere between these two figures and probably closer to the lower end of this range.

Some terraces have circular structures of dry-laid masonry built into their back walls that probably formed part of the domestic complex, but their exact use remains somewhat unclear. Researchers have interpreted circular structures at other sites as temporary shelters, or windbreaks, and associated them with the use of cerros de trincheras as defensive refuges (Fontana et al. 1959; Wilcox 1979). It is unlikely that they were used for these purposes at the permanently inhabited town of Cerro de Trincheras. The preliminary report on Cerro de Trincheras suggested that circular stone structures were used as facilities for large storage baskets for agricultural products. This association is partially based on the ethnographic use of large storage baskets by Piman groups (McGuire et al. 1993:31-2). This interpretation is slightly bolstered by the reported weak tendency for storage vessels to occur with these features at the Tumamoc Hill site in the Tucson Basin (McLean and Larson 1979:92).

However, it seems more likely that these small rooms could have served a wide variety of residential needs and activities. These may have ranged from mundane productive tasks to rituals associated with the domestic group. Two circular rock outlines defined domestic structures with hearths at Linda Vista Hill (Downum 1986). In many cases circular stone structures at Cerro de Trincheras appear to be more substantial than those at Linda Vista Hill. They are also associated with terraces that have large amounts of domestic trash and other indications of generalized habitation. The relative lack of artifacts in circular structures noted during the surface survey could stem from frequent cleaning or somewhat less intensive use of these structures, since many activities may have occurred in exterior areas of the terraces.

The distribution of circular stone structures associated with terraces is relatively uneven across the site. An even distribution of one structure per terrace would mean that approximately 27% of the terraces would have a structure. In reality, only 15% of the terraces have circular stone structures, reflecting the fact that many terraces have multiple structures. Terraces that do not have circular structures may have other forms of domestic architecture, such as the ephemeral jacal structures. This variation may be related to a wide variety of factors, including chronology, composition of residential groups, and other social aspects. The survey data do not provide a clear idea of the range of uses or temporal associations of circular stone structures. Future analysis of excavation data may aid in sorting out the sources of this uneven pattern.

Circular stone structures also occur as isolates, particularly on the crest of the main hill. This is another indication that there may have been variation in the activities associated with circular stone structures. The crest was one of the major ritual areas and circular stone structures here, whether isolates or associated with terraces, were certainly not used for generalized domestic purposes. Circular stone structures on the crest also tend to be larger which may indicate a more restricted purpose.

The social composition of domestic units cannot be accurately assessed using surface information; however, it is not unreasonable to assume that domestic units consisted of some arrangement of kin. Many terraces are not large enough to have reasonably housed more than a small household, perhaps a nuclear family of five or six individuals. A small number of long terraces could have housed multiple nuclear families, extended families, or larger kin groups if they were used for residential purposes.

The general configuration of terraces is also suggestive of larger co-residential kin groups. Terraces at the site tend to occur in larger groupings that may represent supra-household kinship groups. The most obvious terrace grouping occurs on El Borde de Sur, a projection on the southern side of the main hill. Several terraces ring the edge of El Borde de Sur and extend into its center, where a large circular stone structure stands that seems to form a focal point for the group. Most terraces on the southern and western sides of the main hill occur in discrete clusters. Terrace groupings on the heavily terraced northern face are more difficult to define but some clustering is apparent. Clusters on the north face appear to be separated by horizontal gaps in the terrace line, slight changes in vertical elevation, or both. Distinct terrace clusters range from 3 to perhaps more than 20 terraces. This evidence is still tentative but it is not unreasonable to assume that a densely occupied town site, such as Cerro de Trincheras, would have had some forms, or mechanisms, of organization above the household level.

Agricultural Features and Areas

Flotation data confirm that the population of Cerro de Trincheras engaged in corn agriculture (McGuire et al. 1999) and this probably supplied much of their subsistence. Areas near the Rio Magdalena and other washes would have been the most productive areas for maize cultivation. An intensive search for potential agricultural area features was not conducted and, in many areas, modern usage may obscure prehistoric canals and other water control devices. However, there is little reason to believe that the Rio Magdalena and surrounding washes would not have been heavily utilized by corn agriculturalists. Some researchers have proposed that terraces were also used for cultivation (Huntington 1912, 1914; Fontana et al. 1959; Stacy 1974). Recent treatments of the topic have suggested that terraces may have served varied agricultural purposes, including small garden plots and winter cultivation (Fish et al. 1984; Downum et al. 1994).

No specific evidence of winter cultivation at Cerro de Trincheras currently exists. Studies of the agricultural potential of hill side contexts in the Sonoran Desert region have proven that they are superior to valley floors due to their higher average temperatures that decrease the period of frost danger, resulting in fewer freezes (Fish et al. 1984; Downum et al. 1994:282). These researchers also suggest that terraces could have been used to produce a small winter crop before the main growing season. Terraces would augment the natural advantages of hill sides by offering increased protection from frost and radiational heat at night from the surrounding volcanic rock (Fish et al. 1984; Downum et al. 1994:283). The decreased danger of frost on terraced hillsides may also have protected perennial crops, such as chilies, and allowed them to survive for several seasons (Downum et al. 1994:283).

During the regular growing season, prehistoric residents could have also cultivated a wide variety of agricultural products in terrace garden plots (Downum et al. 1994). Archaeobotanical evidence from Linda Vista Hill in the Tucson Basin suggests that corn and yucca, or sotol were grown on terraces. Harvesting and processing tools, such as tabular knives, have also been found at Linda Vista Hill and Cerro Prieto (Downum et al. 1994). Preliminary results from excavations at Cerro de Trincheras have not directly established that terraces were used for cultivation, but flotation samples from terraces do tend to concur with the evidence from other cerros de trincheras. Flotation samples have yielded maize (53% of the samples contain corn), squash, agave, and perhaps, cotton (McGuire et al. 1999). Agave does not currently grow in any frequency on the site or in the surrounding area, suggesting that it was cultivated by the site inhabitants, rather than gathered. Agave grown along terrace edges may have additionally acted to stabilize them (Fish et al. 1984; Downum et al. 1994).

Any of the terrace types (see Chapter Four) at Cerro de Trincheras could potentially have been used for cultivation but one type, narrow terraces, appear to have exclusively served agricultural needs. The 49 narrow terraces are not wide enough to have contained domestic structures. The terraces average 1.95 m in wide, although some are less than 1.5 m wide. Terraces at Linda Vista Hill that are interpreted as agricultural in function based on their size and flotation data tend to concentrate in the mid to upper elevations of the slope (Downum et al. 1994:283). Narrow terraces at Cerro de Trincheras occur at the base of the hill in closely spaced groups of ten or twenty. Rock alignments at Cerro Prieto, which appear to be similar to narrow terraces, also occurred at lower elevations. It has been suggested that alluvium at the base of hillsides would increase agricultural productivity (Downum 1993:85-86). However, these features are located outside the major concentration of hillside architecture at Cerro Prieto (Downum 1993), while narrow terraces at Cerro de Trincheras lie directly below the major concentration of terraces at the site. Terraces up slope may have absorbed much of the run-off, eliminating one of the advantages of a hill base location. One explanation is that narrow terraces at Cerro

de Trincheras pre-date constructions up slope and that their use declined after these terraces were in place.

Researchers have also suggested that site orientation may reflect preferred agricultural exposures. Northeast exposures offer the most mesic orientation in the Sonoran Desert (Katzer 1993:92). Most terraces at Cerro de Trincheras are oriented north or northwest, which have less mesic conditions than northeast exposures, but are still quite favorable (Katzer 1993:92). Agricultural considerations seem to have been only one of a number of factors influencing site orientation, since many cerros de trincheras, particularly outside the Hohokam area, show little or no selection for preferred exposures (Kirk 1994).

The level ground on the southern side of the hill may have contained other, non-terrace agricultural features. Huntington (1914:69) described a series of connecting rock lines in this area that may have been gridded gardens. This is the only mention of these features in the literature on the site and they are certainly not present now. As discussed in chapter three, railroad construction has caused considerable damage on the southern and western sides of the site. Crews robbed rock from this area for use in the construction of the rail berm. Several large, scattered piles of rock in this area may be the remains of the features Huntington (1914) discussed.

Ritual Architecture

Two areas at Cerro de Trincheras appear to have been primarily devoted to ritual activities and performances, the main hill crest and La Cancha. Each has unique architectural features and configurations that suggest specialized activities were performed in these areas. Low artifact density in these areas provides further evidence of non-residential use.

The first aspect of the Cerro de Trincheras crest that suggests ritual or ceremonial use are its distinctive qualities, its location and its prominence. The crest is the place where earth meets sky, a location that may have held importance for agricultural groups in a desert seeking to control, or guide, the agricultural cycle and fertility. The crest is also the only place on the site that is cut-off from the more mundane rhythms of daily life through a trail system that controlled access to the area and this isolation may have contributed to the sanctity of the space and rituals performed here.

The crests of cerros de trincheras frequently have circular to square architectural features that also seem to exemplify the special nature of these locales (Kirk 1994). These features have been interpreted as defensive works but it seems more likely that they are ritual features. Suzanne Fish (1999) has argued that the waist high walls and relatively small size of summit features on cerros de trincheras in the Magdalena Valley would mitigate against their use for defense. These observations also hold true for El Caracol, the summit feature at Cerro de Trincheras, although the walls are higher.

The low density of artifacts on the crest (6.84/ m^2), terrace construction techniques, and terrace arrangement offer additional support for a ritual interpretation. Artifact densities here are clearly not indicative of the intensive utilization associated with domestic contexts. The rock filled terraces typically found on the crest also would not have made adequate residential foundations. Instead, these terraces appear to have been used to augment natural features, create images, enclose areas, and provide viewing places for rites and performances.

Terraces are the primary component within the distinctive flow of architecture across the crest that served to define specific ritual spaces. The westernmost ritual space centers on El Pico de Zopilotes and El Abra Oeste. The augmentation of the naturally triangular shape of El Pico de Zopilotes by terracing can be seen as an attempt to imitate Mesoamerican pyramids and, perhaps,

their symbolic or ritual connotations within the Trincheras area. Whether the constructions on El Pico de Zopilotes are intended to mimic pyramids or not, the occurrence of a petroglyph at the entrance to El Pico de Zopilotes terraces seems to mark this as a sacred context. The eastern terraces on El Pico de Zopilotes overlook El Abra Oeste, which is enclosed by a series of terraces slightly downslope from the summit. El Abra Oeste itself is devoid of architectural features. The demarcated space of El Abra Oeste could have been used for rites and ritual performances, activities that may have been viewed from the terrace area on El Pico de Zopilotes. Alternatively, it could have provided a viewing stand for watching rites performed on El Pico de Zopilotes. Whatever the specific aspects of rituals performed here, the two areas appear to have complemented each other.

El Abra Oeste is separated from El Abra Este, where another complex of ritual features surrounding El Caracol occurs, by another peak. This peak, El Pico de en Medio, has only a few scattered terraces, which primarily occur on its southern and eastern sides. It is quite tempting to view this peak as intermediate space. However, its lack of unique architectural features and arrangements do not support this interpretation. Terraces on the eastern slope of El Pico de en Medio offer the only location from which rites or performances in El Caracol, in the saddle below, would have been visible. But the vantage point here is not ideal since views would only have been partial.

The primary impediment that obscures views of the interior of El Caracol is the height of its walls. The walls of this roughly spiral-shaped feature still stand to a maximum height of approximately 1.5 m. The interior is not spacious, the feature measures approximately 7 by 12.5 m, including the walls, and only a few people could comfortably fit within the interior at any one time. El Caracol's lack of accessibility certainly suggests a dimension of secrecy and control of knowledge surrounding rituals performed here.

There are very few indications of the content of the rituals performed in El Caracol. The interior is devoid of features and few artifacts are found here. However, the shape of El Caracol is suggestive of the symbolic connotations of rituals and their wider significance. The name El Caracol derives from its spiral shape. In Hohokam rock art these shapes have been interpreted using ethnographic analogies with native cultures in west Mexico (Schaasfma 1980:103). There are several symbolic associations for spirals including rain, clouds, corn, serpents of both the regular and plumed variety, the heart, and Grandfather Fire. The spiral is linked to the god Quetzalcoatl, leading back to other elements in this symbolic repertoire through the god's associations with agriculture and water (Schaafsma 1980:90-91). Thus, El Caracol may be related to a general concern with agriculture and fertility, a reasonable preoccupation for a farming population. The feature is also somewhat reminiscent of a shell bisection and this may also signal the symbolic importance or connotations of this material.

The original configuration of features within El Abra Este has been altered. Mining has disturbed some of the eastern peak and the grade school children who constructed the Roman numeral five must have robbed rock from surrounding features. Still, much of the architecture here is relatively intact. El Caracol is the focal point of El Abra Este, and perhaps the entire crest. Several other large circular structures are also located within this saddle (Figure 4.1). How these may have been used within the ritual structure of the crest and why this specific feature type was chosen remains unclear. There also seems to have been some attempt to enclose El Abra Este with terraces and to demarcate it as a distinctive area. This is most noticeable along its southern edge.

The attempts to control knowledge and access to rituals within El Abra Este are to some extent echoed throughout the crest. The limited area and handful of potential viewing terraces on El Pico de Zopilotes and El Abra Oeste indicate that only a fraction of the site population could have actively participated in crest rituals.

Control of access to the crest in general may also have been facilitated by the trail system. The two trails to the summit follow regulated and visible routes. One wraps through a group of terraces on the south face to ascend into El Abra Este. The other begins on the north face and winds its way along the western side of El Pico de Zopilotes emerging on its southern face (Figure 4.1). Terraces on these trails form switchbacks and guideposts that would have forced traffic along a certain route. Anyone ascending these trails would have been clearly visible from trail terraces and the summit. The terrace structure along the trail system may have been put into place to control access to the crest by the resident population. It is possible that the people excluded were enemy raiders and that the trail system was part of the defensive works of the site. However, this explanation does not fit with the architectural data from the crest, which are not generally reminiscent of defense utilization.

The control and limited access that characterize the crest stand in stark contrast to the open and inclusive context of La Cancha. This feature is a broad platform sandwiched between terrace levels at the lower elevations of the north face and roughly at its mid-point (for a complete description, see Chapter Four). At first blush the shape and large open platform of La Cancha seemed to indicate that it could have been used as a ballcourt. Hohokam ballcourts are generally better defined than La Cancha. Several versions of the Mesoamerican ballgame were, and are still, played throughout west Mexico that do not require very formalized courts (Leyenaar 1992). The circular stone structure within the platform, however, would present a major obstruction to ballgame activities. Information on construction sequence is lacking thus, we cannot ignore the possibility that the circular structure is a later intrusion. The ballcourt interpretation can be neither affirmed or excluded based on currently available evidence. In general, it does seem reasonable to conclude that La Cancha was some type of public "ceremonial platform," a designation it first received by Huntington (1914:68).

La Cancha is unlike any other architectural feature on the site. Its size and location are consistent with its use as a ceremonial stage or platform. Cerro de Trincheras has been described as a natural amphitheater (Huntington 1914; Hoover 1941:230). The kidney shape of the hill acts to hold and augment sound to the extent that conversations in the Pueblo of Trincheras are sometimes clearly audible. La Cancha is situated at the center of this amphitheater and there are no natural or architectural barriers that would have blocked visibility. Any activities performed at this feature would have been clearly visible and audible over much of the north face of the site, with perhaps the exception of the highest elevations of the site. Artifact density within the feature is 3.87/sq m, among the lowest on the site. Low artifact densities would be expected in a non-residential area that may have been frequently cleaned for performances. The surface of La Cancha has been bulldozed, which may have moved surface artifacts outside the perimeter of the feature, but exterior areas also have relatively low artifact densities.

Summary of Architectural Structure

Architectural organization at Cerro de Trincheras supports the definition of three broad, general activity categories: residential, agricultural, and ritual. Residential and agricultural use of terraces probably overlapped to some degree. Residents may have cultivated kitchen gardens or a winter crop on terraces adjacent to or within residential precincts. Terraces were the main loci of residential architecture, providing a level base for dwellings and exterior ramada areas. The concentration of terraces on the north face clearly indicates that this was the main residential area of the site, al-though small clusters of terraces on the south face and the western slope may also have served as residential areas. Discrete clusters of terraces may represent supra-household groups, probably organized on a kinship basis, that would have formed part of the social organization and structure of the site.

Ritual architecture affords another glimpse into social relations at Cerro de Trincheras. The crest of the main hill and La Cancha differ in their outward expression of organizational principles. Architecture on the crest is suggestive of the control of the activities performed here, while La Cancha appears to have been more open and accessible. This contrast could stem from a shift in ritual organization at the site. The available surface data do not offer adequate chronological control and the two areas could have been used simultaneously or sequentially. However, the differences between the two areas may be more apparent than real. The crest was certainly a more controlled context, but rituals in both areas may have required the services of ritual specialists who may have formed part of any elite group through their control of ritual knowledge.

SUMMARY: STRUCTURE AND ORGANIZATION AT CERRO DE TRINCHERAS

Artifact and architectural patterns embody a compelling story of the rhythms of daily life at Cerro de Trincheras. It is a story of people engaged in mundane productive tasks, one of exalted rituals that granted them position and spiritual serenity, and most importantly, one that involved them in the web of social relations that structured and enabled all facets of life at the site. It is not a story of people fleeing for their lives against violent assault or surrendering their lives to defensive needs and fear. There is little doubt that Cerro de Trincheras was more defendable than sites located on flat ground. However, the relatively large empty expanses on the main hill and the extremely low frequency of potential warfare related artifacts (e.g., projectile points) recovered during the surface survey (see Chapter Four) indicate that defense and warfare were not paramount concerns.

In place of defense and functional attribution, the complexities and intricacies of the dynamic flow of social relations at the site challenge us. The many functional attributes that can be associated with Cerro de Trincheras that stem from its location, its architecture, and other factors were caught up in this flow. The survey data offer only a glimpse into social relations at the site but this baseline information on the spatial correlates of relational processes and their general form is a necessary first step to more intensive analysis. Many fundamental aspects of social relations and organization at Cerro de Trincheras may have centered on kinship. Kinship is a relatively common organizing principle in non-state societies. In these societies, it delineates access to land, participation in political and ritual life, and in general, forms the bedrock of social life and relations. The clustering of terraces may represent supra-household groups based on kinship principles. This clustering is most evident on the southern and western sides of the main hill and some clustering is apparent on the densely terraced north face. Inferred domestic contexts at the base of the main hill and along La Explanada (associated with clusters 4, 5, and 6 in the total artifact distribution) all encompass discrete groups of terraces. The residential area on the northwestern side of the site (cluster 4 in the total artifact distribution) features two longer than average terraces that may have housed multiple households.

The north face of the main hill was the primary residential area on the site. Both residential architecture and artifacts concentrate here with northwestern areas showing the highest artifact densities. However, other areas on the main hill and in the area surrounding the hill show evidence of residential use. The pit house village to the south of the main hill presents an interesting interpretative problem. If it was contemporaneous with the main hill occupation, then there were two distinct residential patterns used simultaneously. Possible factors involved in the development of differences in residential pattern could encompass forms of social tension and conflict that led to a separation of the settlement or more benign manifestations of social differences. The substantial evidence of residential occupation on the main hill would preclude defensive refuge explanations that would view Cerro de Trincheras as refuge that pit house village populations would use only during times of attack. The cremation cemetery near the pit house village may or may not be related to its occupation. Clearly, better chronological control and excavation data are needed before we can interpret the specific relationship between the pit house village and the main cerro. It is also still possible that further chronological information will establish a temporal separation between the two.

Artifact distributions indicate that some residential areas were more intensively involved than others in lithic reduction and production and shell ornament production. The expedient nature of the lithic assemblage contains little information with which to examine the specific activities related to increased production or higher disposal rates. However, more information is available on the organization of shell production and its distribution.

The basic dimensions and parameters of shell production and distribution at Cerro de Trincheras are clearly established by the survey data. Site residents do not seem to have engaged in intersite shell exchange to any great extent, although a recent comparison of shell from Paquimé and Cerro de Trincheras suggested that Cerro de Trincheras may have been a source for the saucer shaped beads found at Paquimé (McGuire et al. 1999). Most shell ornaments were produced for local, on-site consumption. The shell sample from the surface (n=598) is relatively small for a site engaged in major exchange networks (McGuire et al. 1993; Chapter Four). A recent analysis of survey data from surrounding sites indicates that Cerro de Trincheras was not a primary local source, in general (Vargas 2000). Surface artifact distributions show widely distributed production debris and manufactured pieces. Although certain areas had more of both, it appears that stringent mechanisms of control were absent. Production seems to be associated with domestic contexts, therefore we may reasonably assume that it was principally organized at the household level.

The social and ritual uses of shell make it particularly valuable for interpreting dimensions of social relations, including inequities. Southwestern archaeologists have variously interpreted shell as a socially necessary item that was controlled to a greater or lesser extent by elite groups (e.g., McGuire and Howard 1987) or as a "benign" aspect of intra-village exchange relations outside of direct elite control (e.g., Seymour 1988). The central issue is whether shell provides evidence of "social complexity." This is complicated by the variable interpretation and measurement of the social correlates of production and distribution, the species and items involved, and the scale of analysis. Issues of shell's association with elite status are often further obscured by the terms of the debate. Shell as a "luxury" item is perceived as an either/or proposition. It is seen as either controlled by an elite or not, and if not, then social inequities are absent or not fully developed (Seymour 1988). While issues of elite control are a central component of interpretation, this focus can obscure the intricate dynamics of social relations (McGuire and Howard 1987).

Shell was embedded in numerous and varied aspects of social life and was vital for social reproduction and ritual (McGuire and Howard 1987; Seymour 1988). Evidence of control is not present at Cerro de Trincheras but more intensive involvement in production, or greater access, may certainly have translated into some social inequities. In this situation, differences in involvement and access below outright control may be linked to the ability of social groups or individuals to manipulate social transactions to their benefit, hold more prominent positions within social, ritual, and political organization, or both. The true issue here is how shell and other social valuables were used within differing contexts and how the dynamics of these processes were played out through social relations. An exclusive focus on evidence of elite control cannot capture the subtleties involved.

Social inequalities and differences in social power are also manifested in ritual life and relations, a context in which shell and the symbolism surrounding it may have been associated. Rituals performed on the crest incorporated symbolic aspects of spirals and shell in the architecture of El Caracol, which has a spiral shape suggestive of a shell bisection. This juxtaposition provides an impression of the potential links between shell, ritual, and power. Power and authority are evident in the coordinated effort required to construct features on the crest and La Cancha, as well as in the controlled access to those areas. However, power and authority probably did not reside exclusively in the ritual domain. Ritual relations are intricately bound to other social and political relations and power may have suffused this entire network.

The information we can glean from the surface survey data regarding social relations forms one layer of interpretation in the process of reconstructing the web of relations at Cerro de Trincheras. It is, admittedly, a broad interpretation that provides little insight into micro-scale processes within households. However, it does convey a sense of daily life and a more developed impression of community organization and power relations. The complexities of daily life at Cerro de Trincheras were shaped by, and at the same time influenced, broader scale relations. It is only by considering how community level relations were connected to these broader relations that we can begin to grasp the totality of the site context. The reconstruction of the relational context of Cerro de Trincheras has implications for understanding the role of cerros de trincheras in Northwest/Southwest prehistory. Broader interpretative layers, which consider the significance of the functions and role of Cerro de Trincheras within a multi-scalar relational framework, are taken up in the following chapter.

Chapter Six
Synthesis and Conclusions

The 1991 surface survey of Cerro de Trincheras is one of a number of recent research projects that are shedding light on the complexities of cerros de trincheras. The one common theme that unites this research is the residential use of cerros de trincheras (Downum 1986, 1993; Hard and Roney 1999; Roney 1999). It has become increasingly clear that at least large cerros de trincheras were villages or towns that served a wide variety of needs for site residents. This has challenged functionalist arguments that impute specialized roles to the site type, but has not yet erased lingering functionalist perceptions. To understand the dynamics of individual site histories, as well as the variability within the site type, we must transcend theories that collapse causality and function and look to the real "cause" of cerros de trincheras, that is, human agency as it is embedded within social relations. Agents, social groups, and social relations exist at and draw on multiple spatial and temporal scales, creating many layered textures (Crumley and Marquardt 1987; Crumley 1987, 1995; Marquardt 1992). It is within these textures, and not oversimplified or distorted broad scale models, that the true history of Cerro de Trincheras and cerros de trincheras lies.

Interpretations of Cerro de Trincheras and the Trincheras Tradition were submerged for many decades under the mantle of functionalist assumptions and the implications of the Gladwinian model (Wilcox 1980:239-40). The hierarchical tenets of this ethnic core-periphery model extended to the Trincheras Tradition through substantive connections in material culture, the most visible of which were cerros de trincheras sites. Gladwin's (1928; Gladwin and Gladwin 1929a) theories on the Salado invasion of the Phoenix Basin core led not only to the extension of the "degenerate remnant" explanation of peripheral development to the Trincheras Tradition (Sauer and Brand 1931) but also influenced explanations of cerros de trincheras sites as defensive (e.g., Johnson 1960).

The entanglement of the Gladwinian model and functionalist perceptions of cerros de trincheras resulted in mutually reinforcing concepts that focused on broad-scale factors. In doing so, they created reductionist explanations that ignored local history and process, effectively turning the Trincheras Tradition and cerros de trincheras into "blank" space. Blank spaces are areas of powerless populations that have no history apart from that given to them by an innovative core. In these spaces, broad-scale factors impinge on social life rather than become a part of it. Conceived of as a "blank" space, the Trincheras Tradition did not progress culturally but accepted core innovations. Interpretations of cerros de trincheras represented the sites as a cookie-cutter phenomenon.

The Gladwinian model is losing its potency. Research on the Trincheras Tradition is no longer oriented toward broad-scale issues of cultural affiliation or theories and models that view it as an inferior manifestation of the Hohokam (Sauer and Brand 1931; Haury 1950). The current challenge is to fill the "blank" space of the Trincheras Tradition and cerros de trincheras with new information on local development. The new data being generated is providing substantive reasons to reject functionalist perceptions of causality that limit understanding and constrain theoretical insights.

REPUDIATING FUNCTIONALISM

Functionalist approaches have always rested on the "unique" characteristics of cerros de trincheras, principally architectural terracing and their occurrence on isolated hills. The fascination with terraces is evident in some of the earliest explanations, for example, Huntington's (1912, 1914) interpretation of agricultural use of terraces at Cerro de Trincheras, which invoked their supposed narrow size and lack of dense middens. The emphasis on terraces has continued to the recent present with Wilcox's (1979) detailed analysis of their defensive aspects at Tumamoc Hill. Hill contexts are equally crucial for most functional propositions. Terracing on hills is the definitive expression of the site type and its equation with specialized functions has been the basis of claims for a larger functional and causal unity within the site type.

Data from Cerro de Trincheras and other sites have clearly undermined the proposition that terraces served specialized functions. Analysis of surface evidence indicates that terraces at Cerro de Trincheras served multiple purposes. Residential architecture was the principal component of terraces but a number of terraces also served agricultural needs and were incorporated into ritual space. Residential and agricultural use of terraces has also been well documented through excavation at Tucson Basin sites (Downum et al. 1994) and at Cerro de Trincheras (McGuire and Villalpando 2000). Structures have not been located on terraces at Cerro Juanaqueña, in northwest Chihuahua, but domestic items such as metates, manos, and faunal remains seem to indicate domestic usage (Hard and Roney 1999). These data demonstrate that terraces should not be viewed as imparting "unique" qualities to the site type that equate with special, or limited, uses. The basic function of a terrace was to create a flat platform on a hillside (Kirk 1994; McGuire 1998; Roney 1999), on which a variety of activities could

have occurred. Specific terrace function can only be evaluated within site contexts.

The location of cerros de trincheras on hills seems to provide compelling support for functional perceptions, particularly the defensive association that continues to be used as an explanation for the site type (Wilcox 1979, 1989; LeBlanc 1999; Wilcox and Haas 1994; Roney and Hard 1998; Hard and Roney 1999). Hills are clearly more defendable than flat, open areas. It is certainly possible that many, or all, cerros de trincheras were built because of a primary need for defense. However, despite recent attempts at theorizing warfare as a chronic condition in prehistory (Wilcox and Haas 1994; LeBlanc 1999), we have little proof that warfare existed where and when cerros de trincheras occur. Few potential weapons have been recovered from cerros de trincheras and we currently have no burial data that might show evidence of trauma and violent death (Downum 1986, 1993; Hard and Roney 1999). This highlights a common functionalist error of equating the "potential for" with the "actuality of." Few cerros de trincheras, or their associated culture areas, are well researched, with the exception of the Hohokam. It is possible that evidence of violence and warfare may yet be documented across a significant portion of cerros de trincheras regions. However, even if significant evidence of warfare is demonstrated, defensive, or other functionalist explanations of cerros de trincheras, will never constitute adequate explanations.

The limitations of explanations based on functionalist perceptions stem from their inability to transcend the links between causality, function, and scale. Function, in and of itself, explains little, and any explanation of why cerros de trincheras were built that simply answers with defense and warfare, agricultural utilization, or ideological and symbolic association is inherently reductionist. Functionalist explanations cannot incorporate the significant spatial, temporal, and morphological variability that we know exists within the site type (Downum 1986, 1993; Hard and Roney 1999; Kirk 1994; Stacy 1974). Wilcox and Haas (1994) and, to a certain extent, LeBlanc (1999) have suggested that we need to investigate warfare at lower levels such as the site or the settlement system. Wilcox's (1979, 1989) views on Hohokam warfare contain some potential to capture the dynamics of this process and its connections to other aspects of social life. However, due to the emphasis on the causal role of warfare in the formation of the site type in these theories, the significance of local level process must ultimately be measured in terms of warfare. There is a real danger here of reducing the complexities of everyday life on these sites to the larger battles raging above them. In this sense, functionalist models treat site populations as passive and one dimensional creatures of a determinate causality that overwhelming governs their decisions, actions, and history.

What is true of the defensive interpretations is also true of any explanation that roots causality in broad-scale, functional concerns. The general logic of functionalist explanation is inherently flawed and incapable of addressing significant substantive issues, such as the underlying causes of variability between cerros de trincheras. It is time that we begin to address the real source of this variability—the social relations that bound populations to one another and to their larger material and social worlds.

AN ALTERNATIVE PERSPECTIVE

In this section I would like to apply a relational, multi-scalar approach to Cerro de Trincheras to highlight its explanatory potential. I would emphasize that this is an *initial attempt* and not the final solution. There are inherent limitations to surface survey data and, even though research has accel-

erated, we still know very little about Cerro de Trincheras and cerros de trincheras. It is an exciting time to be working on these sites and every new field season and project has the potential to alter our understanding. The real strength of a relational, multi-scalar approach lies in the flexible conceptual framework that unites local history and process with broad-scale relations, while embracing the realities of everyday life.

A focus on social relations within a multi-scalar framework transcends functionalist thought without losing sight of the significant roles cerros de trincheras may have played within Northwest/Southwest prehistory. It does not abstract cerros de trincheras from their local, regional, or interregional context as "evidence" of some larger process but rather seeks to comprehend the network of ideological, economic, and social relations at various scales. Analysis proceeds through various scales, attempting to preserve the insights gained at each in order to understand how relations intermeshed (Crumley and Marquardt 1987; Marquardt 1992). In this process it may be possible to identify key relations in the developmental trajectories of specific sites. It is also possible to examine how these changed through time as social actors and groups confronted, and acted within the material and social circumstances of their daily lives. These circumstances may have included external threats and hostilities but they also included much more. Any of the functions associated with cerros de trincheras only take on significance through social relations that are the real source of change. Needs for defense, for subsistence, and for sustaining rituals that make sense of the world are expressed and negotiated through social relations. Needs such as these intermesh, transform and become part of the consensus, conflicts, and contradictions that form the basis of social life and change. Thus, the goal is not to identify a single causal function, or even a limited number of such functions, but to explain the dynamics of social relations and evaluate their importance for social life and change. This will provide comprehensive accounts of the realities of social life enacted at specific cerros de trincheras and an ability to compare their key relations. It is unlikely that explanations based on this framework will arrive at a single interpretation of cerros de trincheras. They will, however, illuminate the mechanisms involved in the construction of this spatially and temporally diverse tradition, and how they were transformed and reinterpreted within relational contexts.

If the goal is to understand variability within the site type and to fully appreciate the rhythms of social life on cerros de trincheras, then a relational, multi-scalar framework seems to offer the best approach. The key to this approach lies in building individual site contexts and their web of regional and interregional relations.

Building Site Contexts: Cerro de Trincheras

Cerro de Trincheras is currently one of the most extensively documented and studied examples of the site type. Data from two seasons of excavations at the site, while not completely analyzed, support the results of the survey analysis. A recent systematic survey (Fish 1999) has also compiled data on settlement pattern within this section of the Rio Magdalena Valley that can be used to develop the local relational context.

The results of the Cerro de Trincheras surface survey suggest that social organization is best characterized as heterarchical organizational formation. Heterarchical organization implies that hierarchy and equality are united in a dialectical relation where organizational structures, for instance political and religious, can exist simultaneously and in tension. Thus, there can be no singular, overarching structure of power and authority (Crumley 1987). Social relations and organization at Cerro de Trincheras provided multiple structures and forums for the expression and manifestation of power. The specific structure, or form, of

this heterarchical organization is most evident in architectural organization, ritual architecture, and the distribution of shell artifacts.

The clustering of terraces at Cerro de Trincheras indicates supra-household organization, probably based on kinship. Kinship groups would have regulated access to a variety of material and social resources necessary for social reproduction, providing opportunities for inequality in social power within the group. Shell, a potentially valuable resource related to social and ritual transactions (Seymour 1988; McGuire and Howard 1987), does not seem to have been controlled (Chapter Five; Gallaga and Vargas 2000). However, some residential groups or individuals within them, appear to have had more shell artifacts and a higher involvement in production. Given the potential social and ritual importance of shell, this increased access and involvement may have translated into some social inequality.

The most extensive evidence of differences in social power and social equality at Cerro de Trincheras involves ritual architecture. The control of access exhibited by architecture on the crest indicates that ritual was a manifestation of social power. Rituals on the crest, and perhaps in La Cancha, would have required ritual specialists. These social positions were probably invested with power that likely transferred to the individuals or groups who filled them. Both the crest and La Cancha exhibit a general coherence that may have entailed some degree of planning. These large-scale, non-domestic projects would also have involved the organization of communal work parties that would have required oversight by ritual or other community leaders.

A leadership and authority structure above the level of the kinship group is also evident in the general size of the site. Population estimates for the site used a figure of five persons (from pit house figures [Haury 1976; Wilcox et al. 1981]) per residential terrace, assuming that each such terrace had one such house. Dimensional data from Tucson Basin sites where houses were found on terraces were used to derive two estimates of 719 and 422 residential terraces at the site (see Chapter Five). These figures yielde estimates of 3,550 people and 2,100 people, respectively. Both numbers may overestimate the actual site population, since they assume contemporaneous occupation of all potential residential terraces, but they do provide some index of size. It is not unreasonable to assume that the maximum population at the site was in the range of 1,000-2,000 individuals (McGuire et al. 1993:73). A site of this size would have required some organizational mechanisms at the community level that would have entailed differences in social power and social inequality.

The intersection of kinship, ritual, and other social dimensions with household and community organization would have afforded multiple contexts and relations for the expression of social power. The competing and interlocking demands, interests, and powers of households, kinship groups and their leaders, community, and ritual leaders would have comprised a complex, relational dynamic. This dynamic was egalitarian and hierarchical (e.g., McGuire and Saitta 1996). For example, kinship and ritual would have underwritten social and community solidarity. The enactment of rituals that drew on and created community beliefs and cultural traditions would have bound people together. Ritual and kinship also involved social power and created and maintained social inequality through their roles in regulating access to material and social resources and knowledge.

The differences in power at the community level are magnified when we consider the role of Cerro de Trincheras within the larger settlement system and, probably, in the larger region. Among its contemporaries, Cerro de Trincheras is the largest site, and there is little doubt it was a regional center. An apparent population influx into the local area after its construction (Fish 1999) attests to the probable importance of Cerro de Trincheras in the surrounding region. The power of Cerro de Trincheras within the surrounding landscape is visibly expressed by its monumental proportions.

Cerro de Trincheras is a monstrous visual symbol (Fletcher, in Rathje and Schiffer 1980:294, 347). This visual impact is achieved through a combination of the natural hill, which rises over 150 m out of the surrounding plain, dwarfing all adjacent hills, and the cultural terracing of the site, which can be seen from a distance of nearly 20 km. The choice of this hill and the cultural elaboration of the site through the closely packed terraces on its north face were not random acts. While we may never fully know the specific intention(s) that underlie the creation of this site, it seems to convey an impression of power within the landscape (McGuire 1998). Monumental architecture has similar connotations of visual impact and power. In this vein it is worth reconsidering Haury's (1976) idea that cerros de trincheras, in particular Cerro de Trincheras, were intended to mimic Mesoamerican pyramids. Haury suggests that the sites were a form of "cheap" monumentality that took advantage of a natural hill to produce the height and effect of monumental constructions.

Archaeologists typically consider and assess monumental architecture in terms of labor investment and centralized planning, equating these measures with complexity and hierarchical organization (e.g., Earle 1987; Johnson 1989). Cerro de Trincheras could only be seen as an ambiguous case in these terms. A labor estimate for Cerro de Trincheras yielded a figure of 634,856 person hours or 79,341 person days (Appendix B). The estimate is based on Lekson's (1986) figures for masonry construction and other construction tasks and includes labor involved in fill excavation and terrace wall construction. It is unlikely that the use of trash fill would amount to a significant decrease in this figure, since trash is usually allowed to decompose before its reuse in construction (Schiffer 1987) and would still require excavation and transport (see McGuire et al. 1993:73-74). This estimate is roughly comparable to the labor involved in the construction of a 600 to 700 room pueblo (McGuire et al. 1993:73-74). It is also comparable to some mounds in the southeastern United States such as Mound Bottom and Pack, although it pales in relation to the labor involved in the truly massive monumental constructions at such sites as Cahokia, Kincaid, and Moundville (Muller 1999). The Southeastern data certainly places Cerro de Trincheras within the realm of contenders in terms of labor investment. However, there is no evidence of planning beyond that exhibited on the main hill crest and in the citing of La Cancha to take advantage of the natural, amphitheater quality of the hill. But neither the crest or La Cancha seem indicative of a high degree of centralized coordination. More importantly, Cerro de Trincheras was a town. Most of its architecture was oriented toward domestic life and not the display of elite power and control.

The question of is it or is it not monumental with regard to the measures of labor investment and centralized planning at Cerro de Trincheras obscures more fundamental issues of how this visually impressive site came to have significance in a cultural landscape. Centralized planning and labor investment are hallmarks of the evolutionary approach to monumental construction that seeks to measure sociopolitical complexity. Labor investment has been increasingly criticized as a poor measure of complexity. Researchers note that actual labor investments per capita may not represent significant sacrifices, or control, and that even small-scale societies are capable of erecting monumental constructions (Muller 1999; Earle 1987; see also Erasmus 1965; Adams 1967). Estimating centralized planning is a notoriously subjective endeavor. While we may still be able to say with some certainty that what counts as monumental architecture at Teotihuacan may not mean the same thing at a small, one mound center in the Southeast U.S., this is not all, or even what, we might want to say. Preoccupation with questions of labor investment and centralized planning obscures the issue of how places came to have significance in a cultural landscape. The true power of monumental architecture and other aspects of the cultural landscape lies as much in the dynamics of the relations that gave them meaning and significance as it does in the labor involved in their construction (Kehoe 2000). In this sense, Cerro de Trincheras is a meaningful, powerful place within the cultural landscape, whether it is "monumental" or not.

The power of Cerro de Trincheras within the cultural landscape is clearly signaled by its incredible visual impact. Here again, however, we meet the issue of Cerro de Trincheras as a monumental construction. Visual impact is one of the most salient features of monumental constructions, a quality that is only indirectly measured by labor investment. The visual impact of a construction was a direct expression and reinforcement of the message the builders wished to convey and is more closely linked to actual prehistoric use and significance (Trigger 1990). Based on this criterion, Cerro de Trincheras is a monumental construction. The use of the natural hill circumvents the need for the "piling behavior" (the amassing of large piles of earth, stone, etc.) that is necessary to evolutionary interpretations that focus on degree of labor control (Johnson 1989).

The message of this example of "cheap" monumentality based on labor investment, may ultimately trace back to elite groups at Cerro de Trincheras conveying their power within the landscape (cf. Trigger 1990). Although we currently have little evidence of a significant degree of coercive power over economic or social life by elites at Cerro de Trincheras or within the region (Vargas 2000), this situation may change as research progresses. It is possible that the heterarchical situation outlined above extended to the larger area. Cerro de Trincheras, and any elite groups there, may have been involved in a complex web of ideological, social, and economic relations that were at once hierarchical and egalitarian. Any elite groups at Cerro de Trincheras may have had a prominent role in some organizational aspects within the larger area but this may not have extended to significant coercive control and power over groups at smaller sites. Alternatively, control and power may have been limited to specific organizational aspects. One facet in which the prominent role of Cerro de Trincheras and its population is evident is ritual organization, and here the message of power that the site conveys transforms and intertwines with symbolic aspects to become something more than simply a representation of power.

Suzanne Fish (1999) has proposed that communal ritual observances that may focus on summit features at contemporary, smaller cerros de trincheras in the local settlement system were more complexly enacted at Cerro de Trincheras, indicating ritual ties between these sites. The association of El Caracol, the summit feature at Cerro de Trincheras, and the crest in general, with the creation and maintenance of social inequality presents some tantalizing suggestions regarding the character of these ties and the role of social power within the larger settlement system. The rituals performed in La Cancha appear to have been more inclusive, although they still may have involved the control of ritual knowledge. If El Caracol and La Cancha are contemporary, it would indicate a complex ritual network that may have both integrated populations within the larger area and formed the basis for differences in power, with Cerro de Trincheras occupying a leading role as a ritual center. Alternatively, the ritual architecture at Cerro de Trincheras may indicate a transformation within the ritual network. In either case, it is possible that the manipulation of this ritual network by residents of Cerro de Trincheras, particularly any social elites, was intricately involved in the expression of social power within the larger area. The rituals performed within El Caracol seem to have drawn on themes of agriculture and fertil-

ity, at least in part, which is suggested by the symbolic associations of its spiral shape. The promise of security, renewal, or other aspects these themes entail would have been significant concerns that could easily lend themselves to manipulation.

The placement of ritual features at the apex of hills, at the place where earth meets sky, seems to indicate that hills in general may have held symbolic significance within the context of these ritual activities. There is an interaction here, a relationship between the natural qualities of the hill and the cultural intentions of its occupants. The ethnohistoric record offers some support for the idea that hills held symbolic significance as sacred spaces. Underhill (1946:38) states of the five hundred songs she collected during her study of Tohono O'odham ritual that many of these songs "seem no more than rearrangements of the beloved words 'rain,' 'wind,' and 'mountain.'" Mountains and hills often occur in these songs as landmarks, residences of the gods, or in association with water related words. In a land of endless expanses of flat topography punctuated by mountains and hills, we should not wonder that these dramatic landscape features achieved symbolic significance.

The extent of the ritual network is still an open question. However, other relationships are clearer. Although there is evidence suggesting a relationship between Cerro de Trincheras and Casas Grandes through shell exchange (McGuire et al. 1999), current data does not indicate a high level of involvement in interregional resource exchange. Data on exotic ceramics also indicate that Cerro de Trincheras may not have had extensive contact with groups farther north in Arizona producing Gila Polychrome, including the Phoenix Basin (Gallaga 1997).

The lack of evidence suggesting contact with the Phoenix Basin population may indicate a boundary associated with hostilities. This may be where any defensive needs the site may have served enter the picture. One interpretation of interregional interaction posits that Trincheras, Tucson Basin and Papagueria populations underwent a slow process of ethnogenesis linked to the rise of the Phoenix Basin Hohokam and their attempts to dominate adjacent populations. In this interpretation, an O'odham "ethnic group" is opposed to the Phoenix Basin and other northern polities within the Salado interaction sphere, which developed with the major qualitative transformation of the Classic Period (McGuire 1991). The ethnogenesis interpretation includes Cerro de Trincheras. It is now clear, however, that some Tucson Basin sites predate the beginning of ethnogenesis in the area (P. Fish, personal communication 1999). Warfare is a complex process and its occurrence and intensity would have varied through time and space with shifts in alliances and other circumstances.

The relational context of Cerro de Trincheras currently presents a complicated picture where ritual, power, the visual impact of the site, and the symbolic all mesh within social relations to create and maintain social inequities at multiple scales. It is through these relations that these aspects translated into the realities of everyday life, realities that may have included competing and overlapping interests and powers. Power would have flowed through kinship and other forms of group and community organization. I have focused on ritual and the symbolic in this summary but it is clear that they formed only one part of the complexities of daily life at Cerro de Trincheras. Ritual needs did not *cause* the occupation and terracing of this hill anymore than defense and should not be privileged in interpretation. Defense may have played a role in the development of social life at the site and in the larger area. Understanding the significance of ritual, symbol, defense, or other factors requires the examination of how they were implicated in the dynamics of social relations at various scales. Current evidence contains the most detail on how ritual was linked to relations at both the site and within the local settlement system. Any defensive aspects surely had social implications, perhaps

leading to differences in social power and inequality but there is very little direct information on its role. As we collect more data from Cerro de Trincheras, insights into how the material and social circumstances that shaped the site through their entanglement within social relations will grow and transform.

SOME FINAL THOUGHTS

Although the data to undertake a thorough analysis of the web of relations at Cerro de Trincheras are not currently available, the reconstruction presented here highlights some of the insights that can be gained through the application of the multi-scalar, relational approach. It now seems clear that the site type may stem from the interplay of multiple factors, including defensive needs (McGee 1896; Sauer and Brand 1931; Hoover 1941; Fontana et al. 1959; Johnson 1960; Wilcox 1979; Bowen n.d.; Wilcox and Haas 1994; Wallace 1995; LeBlanc 1999; Roney and Hard 1998; Hard and Roney 1999), agricultural advantages (Huntington 1912, 1914; Fish et al. 1984; Katzer 1993), and the symbolic associations of hills (O'Donovan 1997). Summit features, probably of a ritual nature, are frequently cited as one of the defining characteristics of cerros de trincheras, although they are not present on all sites. However, Cerro de Trincheras was about much more than ritual, agriculture, or defense. It was about the flow of social life and the relations through which social life is embodied through history. A focus on broad-scale similarities, such as found in functionalist explanations, overestimates the degree of unity within cerros de trincheras and subsumes human agency and history under a determinate causality. Site populations would have drawn on and reinterpreted factors and circumstances in accordance with the dynamic context of local social relations. Thus, the goal should be to reconstruct these relations in order to understand how they created both the similarities and the divergences within the site type. The interpretation of cerros de trincheras derived from this analytical approach may never provide a single answer to the question of why people chose to live on hills, but it yields a fuller understanding of the processes involved. Most importantly, it connects interpretations of cerros de trincheras to the flow of social relations, local process, and history. It is surely time that we embrace the real space of Cerro de Trincheras and cerros de trincheras instead of the "blank" space of hierarchical or deterministic broad scale models and theories.

Appendix A
Surface Artifact Analysis

Randall H. McGuire, Maria Elisa Villalpando C.,
Maria O'Donovan, and Jim Holmlund

We collected over 24,000 artifacts from the surface of Cerro de Trincheras. This gives us the largest controlled surface collection from a Trincheras Tradition site and one of the largest ever collected from a cerro de trincheras. We divided this material into the traditional categories of analysis used by archaeologists in northwest Mexico: ceramics, lithics (ground stone, chipped stone), and shell. Our analyses sought to explore stylistic and functional variation in these artifacts for the purposes of dating Cerro de Trincheras and answering questions about its function.

CERAMICS

Sherds from each collection unit were classified into sets by ceramic type and vessel form; for example, Trincheras Plain jars is one set. We analyzed 21,172 sherds with a total weight of 41.31 kg (Table 4.3). Of this total, 20,431 sherds weighing 31.942 kg came from controlled collection units (Table A.1; In the analysis presented in Chapter Five, these artifacts form part of the unit sample, which also includes artifact units that were counted but not collected.), and the remainder were from general collections. The analyses that we present here are based on the controlled collection unit sample, with the exception of the polychromes which included grab bag samples and controlled collections units.

Generally, the sherds that we recovered were quite small. They averaged about 4 cm in diameter and 1.9 g. The small size of the sherds results from firing, trampling, and looting. The ejido of Trincheras uses the site area for cattle grazing, a common practice since the first European settlement in the area. We observed locals and visitors on the site on a daily basis. Many people in town showed us handfuls of larger sherds they had collected on the hill. Additionally, most of the pottery was not well-fired and is easily broken. The small size of the sherds made it difficult for us to identify vessel forms and ceramic type for the collection.

Variables Recorded

We recorded count and weight, in grams, for each set of sherds. All statistical and comparative analyses of the ceramics were based on sherd weight. We feel that sherd weight provides a more representative measure of ceramic frequency than count. Sherd counts can be strongly affected by site formation processes, such as erosion which differentially displaces sherds or by trampling by animals, that break sherds thus inflating the count (Schiffer 1987). For example, unknown plainware makes up 58% of the sample by count but only 37% by weight. All of the ceramics found at Cerro de Trincheras are earthenwares with similar density and composition, so that all types have approximately the same weight per volume. A regression analysis of sherd count by sherd weight (sherd weight = 0.082 x sherd count + 15.68) indicated that only about 50% of the variation in sherd weight between units could be accounted for by sherd count ($r^2 = 0.49$, p < 0.001). Sherd counts are provided for comparison with earlier studies that only report counts.

Whenever possible we identified sherds as to vessel form. These determinations were based on rim forms, bases, presence of polishing on interior of bowl sherds, and body sherds that were large enough to infer the general form of the vessel. Sherds were classified as bowls, jars, seed jars, plates, worked sherds, and sherd disks. Bowls have a rim diameter greater than or approximately equal to the maximum diameter of the vessel body. Jars have a constricted rim diameter markedly less than the maximum diameter of the vessel and have a neck. Seed jars are a spherical form with a rim diameter substantially less than the maximum body diameter but lack a neck. Seed jars could only be determined from rim sherds. Plates are shallow, with an unrestricted orifice and a height less than one-fifth the diameter. Worked sherds have one or more rounded edges but are not circular and worked on all edges. These artifacts may have functioned as pottery scrapers. Sherd disks are circular, with rounded edges on the whole circumference of the sherd. Many, but not all of these have holes drilled in their centers and may have served as spindle whorls.

We followed techniques described by Rice (1987:222-224) for determining vessel form. Painted sherds easily lend themselves to form analysis in as much as interior painted surfaces suggest bowls, while exterior painted surfaces and interior surfaces that are not elaborated suggest jars. The few sherds with painted exteriors and polished interiors were assumed to be bowls. Approximately 64% of the painted sherds could be classified as to vessel form. We were not as successful with the plainware sherds. Only about 7.3% of these sherds could be assigned to a vessel form.

In one case a field crew found 400 Trincheras Plain, variant 3 sherds, weighing 4.99 kg, making up most of a single jar, on the surface of terrace 10. In assessing the volume of pottery we recovered in our collections it is worth noting that this one pot accounted for 2% of the total collection by count and 12% by weight.

Ceramic Typology

Where possible we followed established typological categories in our analysis of the ceramics. However, ceramic typology is very poorly developed for northwestern Sonora. With the notable excep-

Table A.1 - Ceramic Types from Controlled Collection Units				
Type	Count	%	Weight (g)	%
Plainware				
Unknown	11757	57.55	11738	36.75
Trincheras Plain 3	8235	40.31	18014	56.4
Late Plain	361	1.77	1845	5.77
Trincheras Plain 1	26	0.13	230	0.72
Trincheras Plain 1a	11	0.05	13	0.04
Trincheras Plain Unidentified	12	0.06	24	0.08
Late Red	6	0.03	15	0.05
Tiburón Plain	1	0.01	2	0.01
Decorated				
Trincheras Purple/Red	7	0.03	18	0.06
Trincheras Purple/Brown	2	0.01	3	0.01
Nogales Polychrome	1	0.01	2	0.01
Babicora Polychrome	1	0.01	3	0.01
Chihuahuan Polychrome	5	0.02	16	0.06
Ramos Polychrome	1	0.01	4	0.01
Santa Cruz Polychrome	5	0.02	16	0.05
Total	20431		31942	

tions of analyses by Hinton (1955) and Braniff (1985), the major discussions of the Trincheras Tradition ceramic typology have been based on collections from outside the Trincheras area (Scantling 1940; Withers 1941; Ezell 1954; Di Peso 1956; Doyel 1977; Jácome 1986). These collections often only contained small amounts of Trincheras ceramics and it is unclear how representative they are of Trincheras ceramics in general. The purpose in these analyses was to understand the variability in Trincheras ceramics in terms of Hohokam or Mogollon ceramics. As a result, many of the named types have never been formally defined, multiple names have been applied to a single type, and different types have been given the same name. Thus, our current understanding of pottery classification and variation for northwestern Sonora remains at a level comparable to that for the rest of the northwest 50 years ago.

In our earlier work in the Altar Valley we attempted to remedy this situation by defining and refining type descriptions (McGuire and Villalpando 1993). Expanding on this, Randall McGuire examined sherd type collections at the Centro Regional de Sonora in Hermosillo, the Arizona State Museum in Tucson, and the Amerind Foundation in Dragoon, Arizona for comparison to the Cerro de Trincheras collection.

The typology for the Altar Valley was applied to, and worked well for Cerro de Trincheras ceramics. There were, however, some notable differences in the plainwares from the two areas. The Cerro de Trincheras material was browner and tempered with gold-colored mica and sand. The Altar Valley pottery is reddish and contains crushed rock temper. It may be worth noting that there was less variation in the plainware from Cerro de Trincheras than in the sample from the Altar Valley. The diversity probably results from two factors. First, the sample from Cerro de Trincheras represents a shorter time period than the Altar Valley sample and therefore less temporal variation. Second, the Altar Valley is on the northern

border of the Trincheras Tradition where Sonoran Brownwares are more common in the assemblage whereas Cerro de Trincheras near the center of the tradition had many fewer non-Trincheras Tradition plainwares.

Plainware and Redware

The survey crews collected a total of 20,409 plainware sherds from controlled units, weighing 31.88 kg. Two types are represented in this collection (Table A.1). Plainware made up 99.97% of the sample by count and 99.5% of the sample by weight. Local redware was less common, represented by only six sherds weighing 15 g (Table A.1). Applying a red slip to plainware created this redware. The sample included sherds from a total of four defined types and some sherds of an unknown type. Full type descriptions for these types can be found in McGuire and Villalpando (1993).

Trincheras Plain

Di Peso (1956:362) referred to this type as Trincheras Red, probably because it often has a deep red surface color resembling a red slip. Polishing often raises a fine float, which when fired is difficult to distinguish from an applied slip. Based on the standard that the term redware should be limited to ceramics that are slipped red, this type is best called Trincheras Plain (see also Jácome 1986:51). It was very difficult to tell if any of the sherds were slipped

Three variants of Trincheras Plain occurred at Cerro de Trincheras: 1, 1a, and 3. The vast majority of the assemblage consisted of Trincheras Plain, variant 3 (Table A.1). In an earlier report to the National Geographic Society we mistakenly identified variant 3 as variant 2. In the Altar Valley we identified Trincheras Plain, variant 3 as "Thin Plain." We did not recover sufficient sherds of this type there to clearly distinguish it as a separate variant of the type Trincheras Plain. Clearly, a gradation exists (i.e., there is continuous variation) between the variants and the distinction between them is somewhat arbitrary (McGuire and

Villalpando 1993). Trincheras Plain, variant 3 resembles Trincheras Plain, variant 1a and Tiburón Plain (Bowen 1976:53-63). However, it is noticeably harder, grayer, and slightly thinner than Trincheras Plain, variant 1a. In the Altar Valley this type occurred in small quantities in association with Trincheras Plain, variant two (McGuire and Villalpando 1993). The paste resembles that of the type Late Plain but Thin Plain is a coil-and-scrape type and Late Plain is paddle-and-anvil. The paste did not, in Elisa Villalpando's estimation, closely resemble Tiburón Plain. We did not find any sherds with very simple designs painted on them. In the Altar Valley we labeled these sherds as Thin Red-on-brown. A larger sample and much more comparative analysis is necessary before the typological position of this material can be clearly defined.

Late Plain

After Trincheras Plain, variant 3 this was the most common type found in our survey with 361 sherds that weighed 1.85 kg found in controlled units (Table A.1). These sherds account for 1.8% of the total controlled sample by count and 5.8% of the sample by weight. In the Altar Valley this type regularly occurred with a redware (Late Red) but not with any painted type (Hinton 1955; McGuire and Villalpando 1993). This was also the case at Cerro de Trincheras.

This type differs from all variants of Trincheras Plain primarily in its method of manufacture. Under superficial examination it looks much like Trincheras Plain, variant 3, but closer examination reveals important differences. Larger sherds of this type commonly exhibited anvil marks suggesting that the type was produced using a paddle-and-anvil technique. This type differs from Trincheras Plain, variant 3 because it lacks scraping marks, has a higher polish, yields thicker sherds, tends to be more brown and yellow in color, and is harder.

This type greatly resembles the late Classic Period plainware of southern Arizona. No clearly accepted name has been applied to this plainware and a number of researchers in the Tucson Basin have questioned the wisdom of characterizing this material in terms of traditional types (Greenleaf 1975:56; Kelley 1978:72-76; Masse 1980:112-113; Jácome 1986:52-53; Heidke 1986). These researchers either have found the variation in the plainware too great to fit into types or have been asking questions that require a more sophisticated analysis of attributes rather than types.

The material labeled Late Plain here clearly falls within the range of variation that characterizes Classic Period plain brownware in southern Arizona. A far more extensive comparative analysis would be necessary to determine if this material most closely resembles the Sells Plain of the Papagueria or Paloparado Plain of the middle Santa Cruz River Valley. In the Altar Valley we called these sherds Late Plain because they occur in the late prehistory of the region. We use the label as a term of convenience and it is not intended to be a formal type designation.

Late Red

This is a red slipped version of Late Plain. The slip is always polished but less than half of the sherds exhibit patterned polish striations. Polish striations on rim sherds occur near the lip of the vessel that run down the vessel at a 90° angle from the neck band. Many of the sherds exhibited dark black fire clouds but it is impossible to tell from the sherds if they were part of a decorative pattern as occurs on the Hohokam Classic Period types Gila Red and Salt Red. We only found six sherds of this Late Red at Cerro de Trincheras, 1 bowl and 5 jars. Our Late Red would probably be typed as Sells Red in southern Arizona.

Tiburón Plain

We found one sherd of this very thin ceramic type. It is generally associated with Seri sites on the coast of Sonora (Bowen 1976; Villalpando 1988).

Unknown Plain

In addition to the plainware and redware types described above, 11,757 sherds weighing 11.74 kg. were classified as unknown (Table A.1). All of these sherds appeared from visual inspection to be made from local clays. Almost all of the sherds placed in this category were too small to be confidently placed in one of the types. They averaged 1 g and were generally no larger than 2.5 cm in diameter.

Painted Pottery

We found very little painted pottery at Cerro de Trincheras. The field crews gathered 42 painted sherds weighing 183 g, from all collection units (Table 4.3). Approximately 50% of these sherds (n=22) came from controlled collections (Table A.1). From controlled collection units only 0.1% by count and 0.2% by weight were painted. Decorated sherds consisted of Trincheras Tradition types as well as types from southern Arizona and northwestern Chihuahua.

Trincheras Tradition painted types are poorly understood. The existing types are based on small samples of sherds and a few whole vessels. Almost all of these samples were excavated from sites in southern Arizona, north of the Trincheras Tradition area (Scantling 1940; Withers 1941; Ezell 1954; Di Peso 1956; Doyel 1977; Jácome 1986). The collection from the Altar Valley Project did little to correct this situation. We found no painted whole or partial vessels. Regrettably, most of the painted sherds that we found in the Altar Valley were highly eroded and were usually identifiable only by a few flecks or traces of purple paint. The present sample of painted sherds from Cerro de Trincheras is too small to shed light on these types.

Trincheras Purple-on-red

The painted pottery of the Trincheras Tradition is quite distinct, consisting of purple paint applied to a red body. This thick, friable purple paint often contains tiny specks of specular hematite that sparkles when a sherd is turned in the sunlight. Specular hematite suitable for the manufacture of such paint occurs throughout the Santa Teresa mountains and in its drainages into the Altar Valley. Even when the specular hematite is not visible in the paint both the paint color and the body color (same as Trincheras Plain, variant 1) are clearly distinguishable from either Hohokam Buffware or the southern Arizona red-on-brown types.

The tendency has been to lump all purple-on-red pottery into a single type, Trincheras Purple-on-red. Gladwin and Gladwin (1929a:121) apparently saw affinities between Trincheras Purple-on-red pottery and the Hohokam because they called it Sonoran Red-on-buff. Sauer and Brand (1931:107-110) discussed this pottery, which they called Trincheras Purple-on-red ware, and described its distribution as throughout northern Sonora to the east of the Río Sonora, and north across the international border in the Santa Cruz valley. Purple-on-red pottery appears fairly commonly as a trade ware into southern Arizona. Withers (1941:36-40) provided the first formal type description for the type Trincheras Purple-on-red. Johnson (1960:62-66) formally described the type based on his work at La Playa. Numerous archaeologists working in the Santa Cruz River valley have described Trincheras Purple-on-red ceramics. Fewer than a dozen vessels of this type have been found in the valley (Di Peso 1956:361; Doyel 1977:41-43, 60, 85; Reinhard 1978; Jácome 1986:38).

In Withers' (1941:36-40) initial type description for Trincheras Purple-on-red he distinguished a specular from a non-specular variety. Johnson (1960:65) was the first to note that this distinction was not necessarily the result of the mineral content of the paint but rather a result of surface treatment. Trincheras potters had polished over the paint on some sherds obliterating the hematite, making them "non-specular." All of the Cerro de Trincheras material was non-specular.

Trincheras Purple-on-brown

Bowen (n.d.) has distinguished between an unslipped Trincheras Purple-on-brown and a red slipped Trincheras Purple-on-red. He believes that the purple-on-red sherds are earlier in time than the purple-on-brown sherds. A number of sherds from Cerro de Trincheras were typed as Purple-on-brown (12 sherds, weighing 55 g; Table 4.3), but there was not a clear difference between an unslipped purple-on-brown and a slipped purple-on-red. Some of the brown-bodied material appeared slipped and some of the red-bodied material did also. In both cases the "slip" was the same color as the body and may have been a float. The difference in color may result from atmospheric differences in the firing of the sherds.

Nogales Polychrome

Sauer and Brand (1931:109-110) called a white slipped pottery with purple and red paint from Sonora, Polychrome Trincheras Ware. At Valshni Village near Sells, Arizona Withers (1941:40-42) defined a different pottery with purple and red paint on a brown body as Trincheras Polychrome. Di Peso (1956:362) at Paloparado in the Santa Cruz valley near Nogales, Arizona called the white slipped pottery Nogales Polychrome. Given that the label Trincheras Polychrome has been applied to two different types (one slipped and one not), this term is probably best dropped and the name Nogales Polychrome used for the white slipped type (see Jácome 1986:42-44).

Nogales Polychrome has a thick white slip with purple and red designs applied over it. On all of the Altar Valley Nogales Polychrome sherds the purple paint was specular and not polished over. At Cerro de Trincheras we found only 3 sherds of this type weighing 25 g (Table 4.3).

Santa Cruz Polychrome

Santa Cruz Polychrome is poorly defined (Sauer and Brand 1931:77; Di Peso 1951:215, 1956:331). Nevertheless, we typed nine sherds to this type (Table 4.3). Santa Cruz Polychrome resembles Nogales Polychrome only instead of having purple and red designs on white, it has black and red designs on white. The type is thought to originate around the Huachuca Mountains and the headwaters of the Río Sonora in southern Arizona. The definition of this type is based on a very small sample of material from Sonora (Sauer and Brand 1931:77) and southern Arizona (Di Peso 1956:331). Di Peso equates this type with the Tanque Verde phase of southern Arizona (A.D. 1150-1300). Santa Cruz Polychrome superficially resembles Gila Polychrome. We found no Gila Polychrome at Cerro de Trincheras. We suspect that the sherds identified as Gila Polychrome in earlier reports for the site are really Santa Cruz Polychrome.

Chihuahuan Polychromes

Our collections confirmed earlier reports of Casas Grandes polychrome pottery at Cerro de Trincheras. We could easily distinguish this pottery from local and southern Arizona wares based on its distinctive fine tan to orange paste. Eight of these sherds were too small to identify to a specific type (Table 4.3. We classified three jar sherds as Babicora Polychrome, and four jar sherds as Ramos Polychrome (Table A.2). Chihuahuan polychromes date to late prehistory, most from A.D. 1250 to 1450.

Discussion

Out ability to draw conclusions on the functional variation in ceramics at the site is limited by the small number of sherds we could identify to vessel form (876 sherds or 4.29% of the controlled count, and 5.28 kg or 16.67% of the controlled weight; Table A.2). Our limited data on vessel form indicate that jars dominate the sherd counts and weights. Fully 80.63% by count of the plainware pottery, identifiable as to form, from controlled collections was jars (10.5 % bowls, 0.3% plates,

4.5% seed jars, and 0.3% sherd disks). Given that water for domestic use at the site would have to have been carried up the hill from below, it is perhaps not surprising that many jars would have been made, used, and broken.

The ceramic types also give some indications regarding the dating of the site. Residents of the Pueblo of Trincheras reported to us that looters had taken polychrome vessels (probably Chihuahuan polychrome and Santa Cruz Poly-

chrome) from the cemetery. All of the polychromes and Late Plain date to late prehistoric times and suggest an age for the cerro and cemetery in the fourteenth to fifteenth centuries. We found no protohistoric ceramic types, such as Whetstone Plain that we found in the Altar Valley, and no historic ceramic types. The lack of these ceramics suggests the cerro was abandoned before the start of the historic period in the mid-sixteenth century.

Table A.2 - Ceramics from Controlled Units by Type and Vessel Form			
Ceramic Type	Vessel Form	Sherd Count	Weight (g)
Trincheras Plain 1	Indeterminate	19	121
Trincheras Plain 1	Bowl	2	41
Trincheras Plain 1	Jar	5	68
Trincheras Plain 1a	Bowl	3	3
Trincheras Plain 3	Indeterminate	7516	13806
Trincheras Plain 3	Bowl	99	392
Trincheras Plain 3	Jar	593	3619
Trincheras Plain 3	Plate	1	18
Trincheras Plain 3	Seed Jar	24	168
Trincheras Plain 3	Sherd Disk	2	12
Trincheras Plain Unidentified	Indeterminate	12	24
Late Plain	Indeterminate	249	995
Late Plain	Bowl	18	99
Late Plain	Jar	84	695
Late Plain	Seed Jar	9	54
Late Plain	Sherd Disk	1	2
Late Red	Indeterminate	1	3
Late Red	Bowl	4	10
Late Red	Jar	1	2
Tiburón Plain	Indeterminate	1	2
Unknown Plain	Indeterminate	11736	11630
Unknown Plain	Bowl	1	10
Unknown Plain	Jar	13	80
Unknown Plain	Seed Jar	7	18
Trincheras Purple/brown	Indeterminate	1	1
Trincheras Purple/brown	Jar	1	2
Trincheras Purple/red	Indeterminate	5	7
Trincheras Purple/red	Bowl	1	6
Trincheras Purple/red	Jar	1	5
Nogales Polychrome	Indeterminate	1	2
Babicora Polychrome	Jar	1	3
Santa Cruz Polychrome	Indeterminate	3	5
Chihuahuan Polychrome	Indeterminate	1	2
Chihuahuan Polychrome	Bowl	1	4
Chihuahuan Polychrome	Jar	3	10
Ramos Polychrome	Jar	1	4
Total		20431	31942

LITHICS

We divided the lithics recovered on the Cerro de Trincheras survey into ground stone and chipped stone. We recovered a total of 2,351 lithic artifacts on the survey.

Ground Stone

We recorded nine variables for each of the 135 pieces of ground stone that we found at Cerro de Trincheras (Table A.3). These were site number, unit, unit type, artifact type, condition, length, width, thickness, and material. Twenty-one percent of the ground stone (n=29; Table A.3) came from controlled collection units, the rest of the sample was from the general collection. The majority of the whole metates were not collected, but were measured and photographed in the field.

Most of the ground stone at Cerro de Trincheras (79%) was made from the bedrock andesite of the hill (Table A.4). Rhyolite was the next most common material (10%); basalt, granite, igneous, and unknown made up the remainder of the sample. Other than the one artifact made of vesicular basalt, all the other stone would have been available within a 20 km radius from Cerro de Trincheras.

We sorted the ground stone using standard Southwestern categories. These included metates, lapstones, stone vessels, manos, and pestles, which may have been used to grind or pulverize materials such as grain, clay, chilies, or pigments. Axes and tabular knives were used to cut or chop wood and succulents. Polishing stones could have been used to polish pottery.

Metates

Most of the 81 portable metates that we recorded fit into the traditional Southwestern categories of flat and basin metates (Woodbury 1954; Martin 1973; Haury 1976:280) but 25% (n=20) of them did not. These 20 metates we classified as concave metates. The 45 flat metates that we found

were usually made from andesite cobbles that had been only slightly modified by wearing down one surface. They averaged 35 x 25 x 8 cm. Each of the five basin metates was a large cobble, averaging 42 x 29 x 7 cm. They had oblong depressions in the center worn down by a mano used in a rotary motion. Concave metates were open at one end with a long concave grinding surface. They resembled trough metates but were not well shaped. They had sloped sides and a curved lip at the open end of the concavity. Concave metates were large, averaging 48 x 36 x 6 cm. A mano would have been used in these metates with a back and forth motion in the concavity, but because of the sloped sides, the mano would not have acquired the faceted end wear characteristic of

Table A.3 - Ground Stone Artifacts by Type of Collection Unit

Artifact Type	Unit Type	Count
Axe-3/4 Grooved	G	1
Lapstone	C	2
Lapstone	G	7
Mano-Probable	G	2
Mano-Square	G	1
Mano-2 Sided	C	8
Mano-2 Sided	G	3
Mano-3 Sided	G	1
Mano-Loaf, 1 Sided	C	5
Mano-Loaf, 1 Sided	G	10
Mano-Loaf, 2 Sided	G	1
Mano-Irregular	C	3
Metate-Type Unidentified	C	2
Metate-Type	G	7
Metate-Concave	G	18
Metate-Concave, Probable	G	2
Metate-Basin	G	5
Metate-Bedrock	G	2
Metate-Flat	C	5
Metate-Flat	G	36
Metate-Flat, 2 Sided	G	2
Metate-Flat, Probable	G	2
Pestle	C	2
Pestle	G	1
Polishing Stone	G	1
Stone Vessel	G	1
Tabular Knife	C	1
Tabular Knife	G	1
Type Unidentified	C	1
Type Unidentified	G	2
Total		135

manos used in trough metates. We found no legged metates.

In addition to the above metates we found dozens of bedrock metates or metates made on large boulders scattered across the western part of the north face of the hill. They rarely appear outside this general location. In this part of the site there was at least one on or adjacent to almost every terrace. None of these metates fell in a controlled collection unit. We only fully recorded two but a series of quick measurements were taken on about 20 others. The grinding surfaces on these metates resembled those on the flat metates, being about 30 cm long and 15 to 20 cm wide. They were only about 2 to 5 cm deep.

We recovered nine small metate-like artifacts. These would be about the right size to fit in a person's lap and are sometimes referred to as lapstones. Lapstones averaged 15 x 10 x 3 cm and tended to be made out of andesite (44%) and from a softer olivine basalt (33%; Table A.5). These stones had been crudely shaped to an oblong or rectangular form and had one or more working surfaces. These surfaces had striations at various angles and sometimes had shallow depressions worn into their surface. These stones were clearly used as hard surfaces to cut, drill, and pierce some presumably softer material. They would have been suitable for use in lapidary work or, more likely, shell jewelry manufacture.

Manos

In defining mano types we used attributes that related to the intended function of the tools and attributes that were a result of use-wear. The different types of metates that we found would have required different types of manos.

Square manos were finely shaped, square to slightly rectangular, and would have fit comfortably in one hand. The one example from Cerro de Trincheras was made from local andesite (Table A.5).

The most distinctive manos at the site were loaf manos. These are large (average, 20 x 10 x 7 cm) manos that were shaped to a domed cross-section and a rectangular plan. They would have been too long to fit in a basin metate and they were consistently longer than the width of the grinding surfaces on the flat metates. These manos would have worked well with the concave metates. All 16 examples of this type were made from local andesite (Table A.5).

Twelve of the manos in the sample had extensive use wear consisting of two (two-sided manos) or three (three-sided manos) well ground facets (Table A.3). All of these were broken in half, but their widths are consistent with those for loaf manos. These manos probably represent well used, or used up, loaf manos. Three of the manos were unshaped oval andesite cobbles with one worn side. These irregular manos (Table A.5) averaged 18 x 10 x 7 cm, well within the range of the loaf manos, suggesting that they may have been poorly made examples of this type.

Johnson (1960) has argued that Trincheras metates match early Archaic Cochise types, in southern Arizona, and that this indicates the Trincheras Tradition had little dependence on agriculture. The large number of flat metates and the basin metates would seem to support this assertion. Johnson's hypothesis, however, assumes that all the metates from the tradition were used to grind seeds for food. This is probably not the case and we think that the flat metates were more likely used in shell and stone bead production rather than to grind seeds.

Table A.4 - Ground Stone Material	
Material	Count
Andesite	107
Basalt-Olivine	6
Basalt-Fine	1
Basalt-Vesicular	1
Granite	3
Igneous	3
Rhyolite	13
Unidentified	1
Total	135

Table A.5 - Ground Stone Material by Artifact Type

Artifact Type	Material	Count
Axe-3/4 Grooved	Basalt-Olivine	1
Lapstone	Andesite	4
Lapstone	Basalt-Olivine	3
Lapstone	Granite	1
Lapstone	Rhyolite	1
Mano, Probable	Andesite	2
Mano-Square	Andesite	1
Mano-2 Sided	Unidentified	1
Mano-2 Sided	Andesite	10
Mano-3 Sided	Andesite	1
Mano-Loaf, 1 Sided	Andesite	15
Mano-Loaf, 2 Sided	Andesite	1
Mano-Irregular	Andesite	3
Metate-Type Unidentified	Andesite	8
Metate-Type Unidentified	Rhyolite	1
Metate-Concave	Andesite	12
Metate-Concave	Igneous	1
Metate-Concave	Rhyolite	4
Metate-Concave	Rhyolitic Tuft	1
Metate-Concave, Probable	Andesite	1
Metate-Concave, Probable	Rhyolite	1
Metate-Basin	Andesite	2
Metate-Basin	Granite	1
Metate-Basin	Rhyolite	2
Metate-Bedrock	Andesite	2
Metate-Flat	Andesite	37
Metate-Flat	Igneous	2
Metate-Flat	Rhyolite	2
Metate-Flat, 2 Sided	Andesite	2
Metate-Flat, Probable	Andesite	2
Pestle	Andesite	3
Polishing Stone	Basalt-Olivine	1
Stone Vessel	Basalt-Vesicular	1
Tabular Knife	Basalt-Olivine	1
Tabular Knife	Basalt-Fine	1
Type Unidentified	Andesite	1
Type Unidentified	Granite	1
Type Unidentified	Rhyolite	1
Total		135

The flat metates stand out from the basin and concave metates in several ways. The flat metates were expediently made from local pieces of stone and on bedrock or large boulders. Over 90% of the flat metates were made from andesite as opposed to 40% of the basin metates and 67% of the concave metates (Table A.5). Only 27% of the flat metates showed evidence of shaping as opposed to 60% of the basin metates and 85% of the concave metates. The grinding surfaces of the flat metates were shallow, poorly defined, ovals.

These differences suggest that the flat metates and bedrock metates had a different function than the basin and concave types. These differences could reflect a casual use of the flat metates for grinding wild seeds but we would expect to find manos for this purpose. Of the 32 manos in the sample, only the single square mano could have created the grinding surfaces on the flat metates. The lack of manos for this metate type and the spatial association of these metates with shell jewelry debitage and the few stone beads we found suggests that flat metates were tools used in jewelry manufacture and not food preparation.

The three pestles that we found were andesite cobbles that had been slightly modified into long, narrow, tools (average, 14 x 8 x 7 cm.) with battered ends. We did not find any portable stone mortars in which these pestles could have been used. We did observe dozens of bedrock mortars where they could have been used.

The one axe was battered, heavily worn, and three-quarter-grooved (Table A.5). Hinton (1954) collected several three-quarter-grooved axes in the Altar Valley with well-formed ridges paralleling the grooves but our axe was not nearly as well made. Di Peso (1956:359) suggested that the nearby site of La Playa may have been a center for the manufacture of stone axes that would have been traded around northwest Sonora and into southern Arizona. Johnson (1960:130) has questioned this suggestion.

Tabular knives are thin pieces of basalt that have been shaped into a rectangular form and sometimes notched, indicating they were hafted. These artifacts are common in southern Arizona and have been sometimes called hoes or mescal knives. It is extremely unlikely that the two Cerro de Trincheras examples were hoes. They exhibited striations parallel to the working edge rather than perpendicular as would be expected on hoes. Indians in Sonora and Arizona used similar shaped tools of stone and metal to cut and shred agave or other fibrous desert plants. This seems the most likely function for our artifacts. One of the Cerro de Trincheras examples was notched and one was not.

The one stone vessel fragment that we found on the cerro would have been shallow, broad, and square to rectangular in plan view with rounded corners. We estimate that the complete specimen was about 12 x 15 x 4 cm. We found no evidence for legs on the vessel. It was made from vesicular basalt. The form resembles *mocajetes* (chili grinders) found in Mesoamerica and crew members with Mesoamerican experience instantly identified it as such. Johnson (1960:120-122) found five of these vessels at La Playa. As he pointed out, they do not resemble Hohokam stone vessels because they are shallower, broader, and less well made.

The ground stone assemblage from Cerro de Trincheras resembles some of our Altar Valley collection but differs greatly from Hohokam ground stone collections. The basin metates from the Altar Valley easily fit within the range of variation for comparable implements from southern Arizona. However, loaf manos and concave metates occur much more frequently at Cerro de Trincheras than in the Altar Valley or southern Arizona. Perhaps more importantly, we found no evidence of well-made trough metates that occur in both the Altar Valley and the Hohokam. We found no examples of drop-ended manos or metates *delgados* (thin metates) like those from the Altar Valley. The stone vessel from the Cerro de Trincheras is like those from the Altar Valley.

Our sample clearly lacks the finely made ground stone vessels and censors so characteristic of Hohokam sites. For example, we did not find palettes that are often associated with Hohokam censors and stone vessels (Haury 1976). Hinton (1954) picked up one stone palette in the Altar Valley at the La Pera site north of Tubatama. This red vesicular basalt palette was rectangular, 16.8 x 8.1 x 1.2 cm., with an incised

border about 1 cm wide. It had a hole drilled in one end and the surface of the palette was not depressed below the border. Near the center of the palette a shallow depression had been worn into its surface with striations running parallel to the depression. Johnson (1960:122-123) describes three similar palettes from La Playa that also have the small depression and striation marks running the length of the artifact. Johnson notes that these palettes do not look like Colonial and Sedentary period Hohokam palettes but do resemble artifacts from the Pioneer period that were identified as palettes. These artifacts have traces of use wear similar to what we have called lapstones in this report and we would have classified Johnson's two examples as lapstones.

Chipped Stone

By comparison to the ceramics and the ground stone, the chipped stone from Cerro de Trincheras was even cruder and more expediently made. In this regard it is like other Sonoran desert chipped stone assemblages, from both north and south of the border in having few formal tools. Our analysis of the debitage from Cerro de Trincheras primarily sought to identify the range of lithic reduction at the site. The tool analysis found few formal tools and reaffirms the expedient nature of the assemblage.

Debitage

The techniques used in the analysis were determined by the needs of the questions asked and the somewhat limited time available for analysis. A typological approach was used for the debitage analysis. All flakes came from controlled collection units. Flakes were divided into four categories as follows.

Cortex flakes exhibit cortex or an unmodified appearance on one surface. These flakes represent the initial flakes struck from a core, or the initial reduction step.

Secondary flakes result from core reduction and core preparation. A striking platform is almost always present and tends to be cortex material, although, less cortex than cortex flakes. The interior surfaces of these flakes exhibit the classic flake attributes with a bulb of percussion, bulbar scar, and so forth. These flakes have a plano to concave interior surface with a convex exterior surface. These were always hard hammer flakes lacking an interior lip on the striking platform. Secondary flakes accounted for 61% of the sample (Table A.6).

Thinning flakes are generally thinner and smaller than cortex and secondary flakes. The exterior surface of these flakes exhibits flake scars while the interior surface has the classic flake attributes of bulb of percussion, bulbar scar, and so forth. The striking platform is small or absent, and when present is often crushed. Biface thinning flakes that are included in this category, are usually thin, expanding flakes with concave interior surface and an interior lip on the striking platform. These thinning flakes are a result of percussion activity of a controlled nature usually directly involved in tool production from a large flake as opposed to core preparation or core reduction. Very few of these flakes were recovered, which may be the result of our recovery strategy. Their small size makes them difficult to see when collecting artifacts from the surface.

Shatter is lithic debitage that is thick, angular, and usually exhibits four or more sides. Shatter does not have the classic flake attributes but flake scars can be present on one or more sides. Shatter results from core preparation or reduction when excessive force is applied in the blow or from natural fractures in the material which causes the material to shatter rather than flake.

Secondary flakes were subdivided into arbitrary size categories of 0-1, 1-3, 3-5, 5-7, 7-9, and 9-11 square cm. We first drew squares of 1, 3, 5, 7, 9, and 11 cm^2 on graph paper and then placed flakes on them. If a flake could be totally contained in a square, it was placed in the appropriate size category.

Chipped Stone Tools

The 347 chipped stone tools from Cerro de Trincheras (Table A.7) indicate an expedient technology. We recorded provenience, tool type, condition (whole or fragment), weight, length, width and thickness. All of the tools except for three drills, a core, a utilized flake, and a retouched flake were recovered from controlled collection units. In addition to flaked tools, hammerstones and cores are considered under chipped-stone tools.

The choice of lithic material for tool production reflects the expedient nature of most of the tools (Table A.7). The prehistoric knappers most commonly used basalt (58%) and quartzite (38%). Other material includes chert, rhyolite, and andesite. The middle Magdalena Valley contains an incredible variety of rock types and none of the lithic material clearly originated from outside the valley.

Hammerstones are fist sized cobbles with usually angular, battered edges along one or more sides. They would have been suitable for use in chipped stone tool production, to manufacture ground stone tools, or to sharpen metates.

Cores made up 8.4% of the chipped stone tools from the survey (Table A.7). Most of the cores were simply irregular pieces of material that had been reduced using hard hammer percussion, without any clear pattern or formal preparation.

Flakes were typed as utilized if use wear was evident along one or more edges, but had not been extensively modified. Utilized flakes were usually secondary or thinning flakes and averaged 3.2 x 2.2 x 0.8 cm. Retouched flakes had been inten-

Table A.6 - Flake Type by Material			
Flake Type	Chert	Other	Quantity
Thinning	2	49	51
Cortical	2	461	463
Secondary	4	1138	1142
Shatter	5	208	213
Total			1869

tionally retouched along one or more edges. These were usually cortex or secondary flakes and tended to be larger than the utilized flakes, averaging 5.0 x 3.5 x 1.4 cm. Utilized flakes were the predominate chipped stone tool type, accounting for 68.3% of the tools and retouched flakes were the next largest type, 14.4%.

We recovered two types of bifacially flaked tools: bifaces and choppers. The single biface was produced by soft hammer percussion. It was fragmentary, with a width of 3.4 cm and a thickness of 1.4 cm. Choppers were large, oval to pointed, hard hammer percussion flaked tools. They averaged 5.8 x 4.25 x 2.2 cm.

Any flake that had been modified to produce a short, sharp point was classified as a graver. We found four gravers. The points of these tools were scarred with long, thin flakes, presumably

produced by applying pressure on the point. Similar tools could be called borers, reamers, and incisors.

Chipped stone tools on which the working edge has been created through unifacial flaking are often called scrapers but in this report the term uniface has been used. Side unifaces were made by chipping one edge along the length of a flake. These tools averaged 5.9 x 5.5 x 2.9 cm. Domed unifaces are round to oval, domed in cross-section, with chipping around one edge. The single example from Cerro de Trincheras was 5.9 x 5.5 x 2.9 cm.

The only formal lithic tools that we found were a San Pedro point fragment and four drills. The San Pedro point was identified by it characteristic side notched base. The drills all had a wide base with a narrow bit. They were not very large and averaged 2.27 x 1.88 x 1.00 cm. The San Pedro point was made out of rhyolite and the drills out of basalt (Table A.7).

Discussion

The range and variation in lithics from Cerro de Trincheras is consistent with that from Sonoran desert habitation sites and does not suggest a limited or special use function for the site. This is the case for both the ground stone and chipped stone.

The ground stone assemblage contains a range of types normally associated with several functions. These include the grinding of seeds (most likely corn in the case of the concave metates), the manufacture of pottery (polishing stones), tabular knives for processing agave, stone vessels for preparing spices (such as chilies), and lapstones and flat metates for the manufacture of ornaments. These functions are consistent with the activities of a habitation site and do not suggest a specialized activity structure at the site.

A similar variety of types characterizes the chipped stone collection. The debitage includes all stages of reduction, with a predominance of

Table A.7 - Chipped Stone Tools by Material

Artifact Type	Material	Count
Biface	Quartzite	1
Graver	Basalt	1
Graver	Basalt-Olivine	3
Flake-Retouched	Andesite	2
Flake-Retouched	Basalt	5
Flake-Retouched	Basalt-Olivine	14
Flake-Retouched	Quartzite	29
Flake-Utilized	Basalt	76
Flake-Utilized	Chert	5
Flake-Utilized	Basalt-Olivine	66
Flake-Utilized	Quartzite	90
Chopper	Basalt	1
Chopper	Basalt-Olivine	1
Chopper	Quartzite	2
Core	Andesite	3
Core	Basalt	9
Core	Chert	1
Core	Igneous	1
Core	Basalt-Olivine	9
Core	Quartzite	6
Hammerstone	Basalt-Olivine	11
Drill	Basalt	1
Drill	Basalt-Olivine	3
San Pedro Point	Rhyolite	1
Uniface	Quartzite	1
Uniface-Domed	Basalt-Olivine	1
Uniface-Side	Basalt-Olivine	1
Uniface-Side	Quartzite	3
Total		347

secondary flakes. Secondary flakes were not uncommonly used as tools. All stages of lithic reduction including the reduction of cores, tool production, and bifacial thinning were carried out at the site. The range of tool types is consistent with the variation normally observed on southern Arizona habitation sites (McGuire and Schiffer 1982:224-253).

SHELL

The shell material we collected in the 1991 season of the Cerro de Trincheras project differs from the shell we obtained in the Altar Valley. In general, the collection includes diverse raw materials and there is great regularity in the form of the objects. We propose that these objects were manufactured locally for local consumption.

On Cerro de Trincheras we encountered evidence for the selective use of raw materials, especially gastropods of the genus *Conus*. We found more decorated *Glycymeris* bracelets in comparison to the Altar Valley sample. We also encountered a large number of small fragments of *Laevicardium* and *Trachycardium* that were ground on the exterior surface. Other genera appear on the site, but not in significant quantities, including *Columbella* and *Thais*. The absence of large fragments of unworked shell on Cerro de Trincheras, and the small size of the unclassified fragments, indicate that raw materials were roughed out at the site of origin and only blanks for the manufacture of specific objects, including bracelets, rings, beads, and pendants, were transported to the site.

The categories of analysis used in the study of the Cerro de Trincheras shell material were: provenience, condition (whole or fragmentary), and modifications that were made to the shells to convert them into ornaments. In general, only the shell beads and pendants were found whole. All of the bracelets were fragmentary, and so the category "condition" is not applicable to this type.

In the modifications category, a gamut of possibilities ranging from unique process to combinations of different manufacturing techniques, were considered. These include grinding, cutting, faceting, flaking, perforation, and removal of the apex and the spiral. The intermediate stages of processing included semi-ground and semi-perforated shells. We found two different decorative techniques, incising and engraving. We think that the artisans of Cerro de Trincheras used different instruments to attain different results in their fine craftsmanship.

Unique categories were used for the bracelet analysis. These categories describe the characteristics of the umbo or the natural margin of the shell, the location the bevel, and the form of the bracelet in section. Measures of the width, thickness, and the diameter of the bracelet fragment were taken. A measurement of length was taken to determine if there was any regularity in cases where separation did not succeed.

In the case of pendants, the form, section, and location of the perforation was described. The artisans manufactured pendants from a large variety of raw materials.

The identification of the raw materials used in the manufacture of shell ornaments was not possible beyond the genus level. The identification of the raw materials used for disc beads was nearly impossible due to the extent of their modification. We recovered beads of less than 5 mm in diameter in our collections.

Bracelets

Bracelets were the most abundant shell artifact category in our sample. They were all manufactured from *Glycymeris* valves that were almost certainly of the species *G. gigantea*. We recorded pieces of shell that were totally ground and sectioned on the end as fragments of bracelets. For this analysis we took measurements of the length, diameter, width, thickness, and weight of the bracelet fragments. Those fragments that had one

References Cited

Adams, Robert McCormick
    1967   *The Evolution of Urban Society: Early Mesopotamia and Prehispanic Mexico.* Aldine, Chicago.

Brand, Donald D.
    1935   The Distribution of Pottery Types in Northwest Mexico. *American Anthropologist* 37:287-305.

    1938   Aboriginal Trade Routes of Sea Shells in the Southwest. *Yearbook of the Association of Pacific Coast Geographers* 4:3-10.

Bowen, Thomas
    1976   *Seri Prehistory: The Archaeology of the Central Coast of Sonora Mexico.* Anthropological Papers of the University of Arizona No. 27. University of Arizona Press, Tucson.

    n.d. [1972] *A Survey and Re-evaluation of the Trincheras Culture, Sonora, Mexico.* MS. Arizona State Museum Archives, Tucson.

Braniff, Beatriz C.
    1978   Preliminary Interpretations Regarding the Role of the San Miguel River, Sonora, Mexico. In *Across the Chichimec Sea: Papers in Honor of J. Charles Kelley*, edited by Carroll L. Riley and Basil C. Hedrick, pp. 67-82. Southern Illinois University Press, Carbondale.

    1985   La Frontera Protohistórica Pima-Ópata en Sonora, Mexico. Tesis de Doctorado, Facultad de Filosofía y Letras. UNAM, Mexico, D.F.

Braniff, Beatriz C., and Cesar Quijada
    1978   Catálogo de Sitios Arqueológicos de Sonora a Enero de 1977. *Noroeste de Mexico* 1:1-39.

Burrus, Ernest S.
    1971   *Kino and Manje, Explorers of Sonora and Arizona.* Jesuit Historical Society, Rome.

Crumley, Carole L.
    1987   A Dialectical Critique of Hierarchy. In *Power Relations and State Formation*, edited by Thomas C. Patterson and Christine W. Gailey, pp. 155-169. American Anthropological Association, Washington D.C.

    1995   Heterarchy and the Analysis of Complex Societies. In *Heterarchy and the Analysis of Complex Societies*, edited by Robert M. Ehrenreich, Carole L. Crumley, and Janet E. Levy, pp. 1-6. Archaeological Papers of the American Anthropological Association No. 6. American Anthropological Association, Arlington, Virginia.

Crumley, Carole L., and William Marquardt (editors)
    1987   *Regional Dynamics: Burgundian Landscapes in Historical Perspective.* Academic Press, New York.

Di Peso, Charles C.
    1951   *The Babocomari Village Site on the Babocomari River, Southeastern Arizona.* Amerind Foundation Series No. 5. Amerind Foundation, Dragoon, Arizona.

1956   *The Upper Pima of San Cayetano del Tumacacori: An Archaeohistorical Reconstruction of the Ootam of Pimeria Alta.* Amerind Foundation Series No. 7. Amerind Foundation, Dragoon, Arizona.

Downum, Christian E.
1986   The Occupational Use of Hill Space in the Tucson Basin: Evidence From Linda Vista Hill. *Kiva* 51:219-233.

1993   *Between Desert and River: Hohokam Settlement and Land Use in the Los Robles Community.* Anthropolocial Papers of the University of Arizona No. 57. University of Arizona Press, Tucson.

Downum, Christian E., Paul R. Fish, and Suzanne K. Fish
1994   Refining the Role of Cerros de Trincheras in Southern Arizona Settlement. *Kiva* 59:271-296.

Doolittle, William, III
1988   *Pre-hispanic Occupance in the Valley of Sonora, Mexico.* Anthropological Papers of the University of Arizona No. 48. University of Arizona Press, Tucson.

Doyel, David
1977   *Excavations in the Santa Cruz River Valley, Southeastern Arizona.* Arizona State Museum Archaeological Series No. 44. University of Arizona, Tucson.

Earle, Timothy
1987   Chiefdoms in Archaeological and Ethnohistoric Perspective. *Annual Review of Anthropology* 16:279-308.

Ekholm, Gordon
1937   Survey field notes from Sonora and Sinaloa. MS. Anthropology Archives. American Museum of Natural History, New York.

1939   Results of an Archaeological Survey of Sonora and Northern Sinaloa. *Revista Mexicana de Estudios Antropológicos* 3:7-11.

Erasmus, Charles J.
1965   Monument Building: Some Field Experiments. *Southwestern Journal of Anthropology* 21:277-301.

Ezell, Paul H.
1954   An Archaeological Survey of Northwestern Papagueria. *The Kiva* 19:1-26.

Fish, Suzanne K.
1999   The Cerro de Trincheras Settlement and Land Use Survey. Report to the National Geographic Society for Grant 5856-97. MS. Arizona State Museum, Tucson.

Fish, Suzanne K., Paul R. Fish, and Christian Downum
1984   Hohokam Terraces and Agricultural Production in the Tucson Basin. In *Prehistoric Agricultural Strategies in the Southwest,* edited by Suzanne K. Fish, Paul R. Fish, and Martha R. Binford, pp. 55-71. Arizona State University Anthropological Research Papers No. 33. Arizona State University, Tempe.

Fontana, Bernard L., J. Cameron Greenleaf, and Donnely D. Cassidy
1959   A Fortified Arizona Mountain. *The Kiva* 25:41-52.

Fraps, Clara Lee
1936   Blackstone Ruin. *The Kiva* 2:9-12.

Gallaga, Emiliano M.
1997   Analisis de la Ceramica Policroma del Sitio Cerro de Trincheras, Sonora, Mexico. Tesis, Escuela Nacional de Antropología e Historia, Mexico, D.F.

Gallaga, Emiliano M., and Victoria Vargas
2000   Spatial Distribution Analysis of Shell and Polychrome Ceramics at Cerro de Trincheras, Sonora, Mexico. Paper presented at the 65th Annual Meeting of the Society for American Archaeology, Philadelphia.

Gladwin, Harold S.
1928   *Excavation at Casa Grande, Arizona*. Southwest Museum Papers No. 2. Los Angeles.

Gladwin, Winifred, and Harold S. Gladwin
1929a   *The Red-on-buff Culture of the Papagueria*. Medallion Papers No. 4. Gila Pueblo, Globe, Arizona.

1929b   *The Red-on-buff Culture of the Gila Basin*. Medallion Papers No. 3. Gila Pueblo, Globe, Arizona.

1930a   *The Western Range of the Red-on-buff Culture*. Medallion Papers No. 5. Gila Pueblo, Globe, Arizona.

1930b   *An Archaeological Survey of the Verde Valley*. Medallion Papers No. 6. Gila Pueblo, Globe, Arizona.

1933   *Some Southwestern Pottery Types, Series III*. Medallion Papers No. 13. Gila Pueblo, Globe, Arizona.

Gladwin, Harold S., Emil W. Haury, E. B. Sayles, and Nora Gladwin
1938   *Excavations at Snaketown: Material Culture*. Medallion Papers No. 25. Gila Pueblo, Globe, Arizona.

Golden Software
1990   *Surfer Manual*. Golden Software.

Greenleaf, J. Cameron
1975   *Excavations at Punta de Agua in the Santa Cruz River Basin, South-eastern Arizona*. Anthropological Papers of the University of Arizona No. 26. University of Arizona Press, Tucson.

Hamilton, Leodidas Le Cenci
1883   *Hamilton's Mexican Handbook*. D. Lothrop, Boston.

Hard, Robert J., and John R. Roney
1998a   Una Investigación Arqueológica de los Sitios Cerros de Trincheras del Arcaico Tardio en Chihuahua, Mexico. Report submitted to Consejo de Arqueología, Instituto Nacional de Antropología e Historia, Mexico, D.F.

1998b   A Massive Terraced Village Complex in Chihuahua, Mexico, 3000 Years Before Present. *Science* 279(5357):1661-1664.

1999   *An Archaeological Investigation of Late Archaic Cerros de Trincheras Sites in Chihuahua, Mexico: Results of the 1998 Investigations*. The University of Texas at San Antonio Special Report No. 25. Center for Archaeological Research, San Antonio.

Hard, Robert J., Jose E. Zapata, Bruce K. Moses, and John R. Roney
1999   Terrace Construction in Northern Chihuahua, Mexico: 1150 B.C. and Modern Experiments. *Journal of Field Archaeology* 26:129-146.

Haury, Emil
  1950 *The Stratigraphy and Archaeology of Ventana Cave.* University of Arizona Press, Tucson.

  1976 *The Hohokam.* University of Arizona Press, Tucson.

Hayden, Julian D.
  1956 Notes on the Archaeology of the Central Coast of Sonora, Mexico. *The Kiva* 21:3-4.

  1972 Hohokam Petroglyphs of the Sierra Pinacate, Sonora and the Hohokam Shell Trade. *The Kiva* 37:74-84.

Hinton, Thomas B.
  1954 Survey field notes from the Altar Valley. MS. Amerind Foundation, Dragoon, Arizona.

  1955 A Survey of Archaeological Sites in the Altar Valley, Sonora. *The Kiva* 21:1-12.

Heidke, James
  1986 Plainware Ceramics. In *Archaeological Investigations at the Tanque Verde Wash Site: A Middle Rincon Settlement in the Eastern Tucson Basin,* edited by Mark Elson, pp. 181-232. Institute for American Research Papers No. 7. Institute for American Research, Tucson, Arizona.

Hoover, J.W.
  1941 Cerros de Trincheras of the Arizona Papagueria. *Geographical Review* 31:228-239.

Huntington, Ellsworth
  1910 Survey filed notes from Sonora. MS. Sterling memorial Library. Yale University, New Haven.

  1912 The Fluctuating Climate of North America—The Ruins of the Hohokam. *Annual Report of the Board of Regents of the Smithsonian Institution,* pp. 383-387. Smithsonian Institution, Washington D.C.

  1914 *The Climatic Factor as Illustrated in Arid America.* Publications of the Carnegie Institute No.192. Carnegie Institute, Washington, D.C.

Ives, Ronald L.
  1936 A Trinchera near Quitovaquita, Sonora. *American Anthropologist* 38:257-259.

Jácome, Felipe Carlos
  1986 *The Nogales Wash Site.* Pimería Alta Historical Society, Nogales.

Johnson, Alfred E.
  1960 The Place of the Trincheras Culture in Northern Sonora in Southwestern Archaeology. Master's thesis, University of Arizona, Tucson.

  1963 The Trincheras Culture of Northern Sonora. *American Antiquity* 29:174-186.

Johnson, Gregory A.
  1989 Dynamics of Southwestern Prehistory: Far Outside—Looking In. In *Dynamics of Southwestern Prehistory,* edited by George J. Gumerman and Linda S. Cordell, pp. 371-390. Southern Illinois University Press, Washington, D.C.

Katzer, Keith
 1993   A Geomorphic Evaluation of the Agricultural Potential of Cerros de Trincheras. In *Between Desert and River: Hohokam Settlement and Land Use in the Los Robles Community*, compiled by Christian E. Downum, pp. 91-95. Anthropological Papers of the University of Arizona No. 57. University of Arizona Press, Tucson.

Kehoe, Alice B.
 2000   Theaters of Power. Paper Presented at the Seventeenth Annual Visiting Scholar Conference, Carbondale, Illinois.

Kelly, Isabel T.
 1978   *The Hodges Ruin: A Hohokam Community in the Tucson Basin*. Anthropological Papers of the University of Arizona No. 30. University of Arizona Press, Tucson.

Kirk, Matthew, J.
 1994   A Comparison of Cerros de Trincheras in the Southwestern United States and Northwest Mexico. Senior Honors Thesis, SUNY-Binghamton, Binghamton.

LeBlanc, Steven A.
 1999   *Prehistoric Warfare in the American Southwest.* University of Utah Press, Salt Lake City.

Lekson, Stephen H.
 1986   *Great Pueblo Architecture of Chaco Canyon, New Mexico.* University of New Mexico Press, Albuquerque.

Leyenaar, Ted J. J.
 1992   *Ulama*: The Survival of the Mesoamerican Ballgame: *Ullamaliztli. Kiva* 58:115-154.

Lindauer, Owen, and Bert Zaslow
 1994   Homologous Style Structures in Hohokam and Trincheras Art. *Kiva* 59:319-44.

Lumholtz, Carl
 1912   *New Trails in Mexico*. Charles Scribner & Sons, New York.

MacMahon, James
 1985   *Deserts*. Alfred A. Knopf, New York.

MacWilliams, Arthur C., and Jane H. Kelley
 2000   A Ceramic Period Boundary in Central Chihuahua. Paper presented at the 65th Annual Meeting of the Society for American Archaeology, Philadelphia.

Marquardt, William H.
 1992   Dialectical Archaeology. In *Archaeological Method and Theory*, Vol. 4, edited by Michael B. Schiffer, pp. 101-140. University of Arizona Press, Tucson.

Martin, Paul S.
 1973   Tools: Changes in Artifact Morphology and Distribution. In *The Archaeology of Arizona*, edited by Fred Plog and Paul S. Martin, pp. 215-221. Natural History Press, Garden City, New York.

Masse, W. Bruce
 1980   *Excavations at Gu Achi*. Western Archaeological Center Publications in Archaeology No. 12. National Park Service, Tucson, Arizona.

McGee, W.J.
   1895   The Beginning of Agriculture. *American Anthropologist* 8:350-375.

   1896   Expedition to the Papagueria and Seriland. *American Anthropologist* 9:93-98.

   2000   *Trails to Tiburón: The 1894 and 1895 Field Diaries of W.J. McGee.* Transcribed by Hazel McGeely Fontana. University of Arizona Press, Tucson.

McGuire, Randall H.
   1985   Las Trincheras Prospecion Proyecto, Trabajo del Campo, Verano 1984. Report to INAH. MS. INAH, Centro Regional de Noroeste, Hermosillo, Sonora.

   1991   From the Outside Looking In: The Concept of Periphery in Hohokam Archaeology. In *Exploring the Hohokam: Prehistoric Desert Dwellers of the Southwest*, edited by George J. Gumerman, pp. 347-382. Amerind Foundation, Dragoon, Arizona.

   1994   *Death, Society and Ideology.* Westview Press, Boulder.

   1997   Final Project Report, Cerro de Trincheras Excavation Project. Report on file at the National Science Foundation, Washington, D.C.

   1998   A comparison of Terraced Settlements in the Southwest/Northwest and in Mesoamerica. Paper presented at the 63rd Annual Meeting of the Society for American Archaeology, Seattle.

McGuire, Randall H., and Ann Valdo Howard
   1987   The Structure and Organization of Hohokam Shell Exchange. *The Kiva* 52:113-146.

McGuire, Randall H., and Dean J. Saitta
   1996   Although They Have Petty Captains, They Obey Them Badly: The Dialectics of Prehispanic Western Pueblo Social Organization. *American Antiquity* 61:197-216.

McGuire, Randall H., and Michael B. Schiffer
   1982   *Hohokam and Patayan: The Archaeology of Southwestern Arizona.* Academic Press, New York.

McGuire, Randall H., and Maria Elisa Villalpando C.
   1993   An Archaeological Survey of the Altar Valley, Sonora, Mexico. Arizona State Museum Archaeological Series No. 184. University of Arizona, Tucson.

   2000   Excavations at Cerro de Trincheras. MS. INAH, Centro Regional de Noroeste, Hermosillo, Sonora.

McGuire, Randall H., Maria Elisa Villalpando C., James Holmlund, and Maria O'Donovan
   1993   Cerro de Trincheras Mapping Project, Final Technical Report to the National Geographic Society for Grant #4454-91. MS. INAH, Centro Regional de Noroeste, Hemosillo, Sonora.

McGuire, Randall H., Maria Elisa Villalpando C., Victoria Vargas, and Emiliano Gallaga
   1999   Cerro de Trincheras and the Casas Grandes World. In *The Casas Grandes World*, edited by Curtis Schaafsma and Carroll Riley, pp. 134-148. University of Utah Press, Salt Lake City.

McLean, David R., and Stephen M. Larson
   1979   Inferences from the Distribution of Plainware Sherd Attributes on Tumamoc Hill. *The Kiva* 45:83-94.

Muller, Jon
1999   The Southeast. In *Great Towns and Regional Polities in the Prehistoric American Southwest and Southeast*, edited by Jill Neitzel, pp. 143-58. University of New Mexico Press, Albuquerque.

O'Donovan, Maria
1997   Confronting Archaeological Enigmas: Cerros de Trincheras, Cerros de Trincheras and Monumentality. Ph.D. dissertation. Department of Antrhopology, SUNY-Binghamton.

Pailes, Richard A.
1972   *An Archaeological Reconnaissance of Southern Sonora and Reconsideration of the Rio Sonora Culture*. Ph.D. dissertation, Southern Illinois University. University Microfilms, Ann Arbor.

1978   The Rio Sonora Culture in Prehistoric Trade Systems. In *Across the Chichimec Sea: Papers in Honor of J. Charles Kelley*, edited by Carroll L. Riley and Basil C. Hedrick, pp. 134-43. Southern Illinois University Press, Carbondale.

Pfefferkorn, Ignaz
1990 [1795]   *Sonora: A Description of the Province*. Translated and annotated by Theodore E. Treutlein. The Southwest Center Series, edited by Bernard L. Fontana. University of Arizona Press, Tucson.

Rathje, William L., and Michael B. Schiffer
1980   *Archaeology*. Harcourt, Brace, Jovanovich, New York.

Rice, Prudence
1987   *Pottery Analysis: A Sourcebook*. University of Chicago Press, Chicago.

Reinhard, Karl
1978   Prehistoric Cremations from Nogales, Arizona. *The Kiva* 43:231-252.

Roney, John R.
1996   Late Archaic Cerros de Trincheras in Northwestern Chihuahua. Paper presented at the 61st Annual Meeting of the Society for American Archaeology, New Orleans.

1999   Canador Peak: An Early Pithouse-period Cerro de Trincheras in Southwestern New Mexico. In *La Frontera: Papers in Honor of Patrick H. Beckett*, edited by Meliha Duran and David T. Kirkpatrick, pp. 173-184. Papers of the Archaeological Society of New Mexico No. 25, Albuquerque.

Roney, John R., and Robert J. Hard
1998   A Note on the Temporal and Geographic Distribution of Cerros de Trincheras. Paper presented at the 63rd Annual Meeting of the Society for American Archaeology, Seattle.

Russell, Frank
1975   *The Pima Indians*. University of Arizona Press, Tucson.

Sauer, Carl, and Donald Brand
1931   Prehistoric Settlements of Sonora with Special Reference to Cerros de Trincheras. *University of California Publications in Geography* 5(3):67-148.

Scantling, Frederick H.
1940   Excavations at the Jackrabbit Ruin, Papago Indian Reservation, Arizona. Master's thesis, Department of Anthropology, University of Arizona, Tucson.

Schaafsma, Polly
    1980   *Indian Rock Art of the Southwest*. School of American Research Press, Santa Fe.

Schiffer, Michael
    1987   *Formation Processes of the Archaeological Record*. University of New Mexico Press, Albuquerque.

Schumacher, Peter
    1881   Ancient Fortifications in Sonora. *American Antiquarian* 4:227-229.

Seymour, Deni, J.
    1988   An Alternative View of Sedentary Period Hohokam Shell-Ornament Production. *American Antiquity* 53:812-829.

Stacy, Valeria Kay
    1974   *Cerros de Trincheras in the Arizona Papagueria*. Ph.D. dissertation, University of Arizona, Tucson. University Microfilms, Ann Arbor.

    1977   Activity Patterning at Cerros de Trincheras in South Central Arizona. *The Kiva* 43:11-18.

Trigger, Bruce
    1990   Monumental Architecture: A Thermodynamic Explanation of Symbolic Behavior. *World Archaeology* 22(2):119-131.

Underhill, Ruth
    1939   *The Social Organization of the Papago Indians*. Columbia University Contributions to Anthropology, Vol 30. Columbia University Press, New York.

    1946   *Papago Indian Religion*. Columbia University Press, New York.

Vargas, Victoria
    2000   Shell Ornament Production and Consumption at Trincheras Sites in the Magdalena River Valley, Sonora. Paper presented at the 65th Annual Meeting of the Society for American Archaeology, Philadelphia.

Villalpando, Maria Elisa
    1988   Rutas de Intercambio Objetos de Concha en el Noroeste de México. *Cuicuilco* 21:77-82.

Wallace, Henry D.
    1995   *Archaeological Investigations at Los Morteros: A Prehistoric Settlement in the Northern Tucson Basin*. Anthropological Papers No. 17. Center for Desert Archaeology, Tucson.

Wasley, William W.
    1968   Archaeological Survey in Sonora, Mexico. Paper presented at the 33rd Annual Meeting of the Society for American Archaeology, Santa Fe.

Wilcox, David R.
    1979   Implications of Dry Laid Masonry Walls on Tumamoc Hill. *The Kiva* 45:15-38.

    1980   The Current Status of the Hohokam Concept. In *Current Issues in Hohokam Prehistory*, edited by David E. Doyel and Fred Plog, pp. 236-242. Arizona State University Anthropological Research Papers No. 23. Arizona State University, Tempe.

1989   Hohokam Warfare. In *Cultures in Conflict: Current Archaeological Perspectives*, edited by Diana C. Tkaczuk and Brian C. Vivian, pp. 163-172. Proceedings of the Twentieth Annual Chacmool Conference. University of Calgary Archaeological Association, Calgary.

Wilcox, David R., and Jonathan Haas
1994   The Scream of the Butterfly: Competition and Conflict in the Prehistoric Southwest. In *Themes in Southwest Prehistory*, edited by George J. Gumerman, pp. 211-238. School of American Research Press, Santa Fe.

Wilcox, David R., and Stephen M. Larson
1979   Introduction to the Tumamoc Hill Survey. *The Kiva* 45:1-14.

Wilcox, David R., Thomas R. McGuire, and Charles Sternberg
1981   *Snaketown Revisited*. Arizona State Museum Archaeological Series No. 155. University of Arizona, Tucson.

Withers, Arnold M.
1941   Excavations at Valshni Village, Arizona. Master's thesis, Department of Anthropology, University Arizona, Tucson.

Woodbury, Richard B.
1954   *Prehistoric Stone Implements of Northeastern Arizona*. Papers of the Peabody Museum of American Archaeology and Ethnology No. 34. Harvard University, Cambridge.

Woodward, Arthur
1936   A Shell Bracelet Manufactory. *American Antiquity* 2:117-125.